I0187316

Life After 25: Intuitively Me

by

Misha Mayhand

Edited by

Ashley N. Holden

Copyright © 2016 Misha Mayhand

All rights reserved. No part of this book may be used or reproduced in any manner whatsoever without the written permission of the Publisher. Printed in the United States of America. For more information
visit www.Ambitiousmixllc.com

ISBN: 10: 0-692-86295-1
ISBN-13: 978-0-692-86295-7
First Edition

Table of Contents

Introduction: No one said it'd be easy… they said it'd be very easy or so they made it seem.

Disclaimer: Throughout this book, I visit several different timelines during my life. I have placed years and timeframes accordingly in hopes that it'll help you follow along throughout my journey of growth. The entire theme of this book is based on the "then and now," of my perspective.

2014

"Go to school," they said. "Education is the key to success," they said. A college degree will get you a financially secure job…blah blah blah. There are people with and without high school diplomas that make more money than me and they get the bonus of not having to deal with student loan debt. What we weren't told is that while education is the key to success, it is not unnecessary to rack up thousands in student loan debt. What I've learned is that there are some things that could have been self-taught.

You may also learn things by shadowing a mentor in the field; these alternatives are less expensive yet equally beneficial. I think what's most overwhelming about this time in my life is the fact that I have yet to see a return on my investment. I attended college for four years only to rack up $33,000 in student loans while obtaining a bachelor's degree and end up making $33,813 a year after graduating. It's said that the picture in our head of how it's supposed to be is what screws us up the most.

I suffer from that. I thought I'd at least be making $40,000 out of college based solely on the fact that I have a bachelor's degree. Having a degree means nothing when you're working in a state with limited work opportunities. My degree is in Journalism with a minor in Communication yet there are no jobs here willing to take a chance on an entry-level journalist and it is even harder to get into the communication department in a company. We're in the age of non-paid internships which creates an issue for those that need the experience but cannot afford to take the internship.

The wealthier peer who comes from a well-off family is able to work for free and can take advantage of those opportunities; They're able to rack up the experience needed to land a job in such a competitive market, thus landing their dream job

right out of college. Meanwhile, your few internships still weren't enough and unless you can move to a less competitive market, which is usually in the middle of nowhere, you're stuck taking whatever decent paying job you can get to make ends meet. Sadly, there are more stories that take this turn than the latter.

I started hearing more realistic stories as I approached the end of my college career. I remember being told that my first job probably wouldn't be in my field of study. Others told me that they never ended up working

in their field of study and took interest in another career path. I see it happening everyday not only to myself but to some of my peers. It can be very daunting if you allow it to be but it doesn't have be that way.

One of my strengths is being able to see the positive in a trying situation. At some point in our lives we must humble ourselves and practice perseverance. If you really want something and you work hard at it, you will eventually get it. Hard work does pay off. Believe me, I'm walking proof of that but how do you stay positive throughout the journey?

I think that's something we all struggle with whether you're a recent college graduate or not. Take a walk with me on this journey of changing my mindset while crossing over from a young lady to a grown woman. A mindset that was forced upon me as I neared my 25th birthday. A mindset that I discovered when my thought process created the crisis that we all experience at a quarter of a century. It is best known as the quarter-life crisis.

Chapter 1

Life...and the Internet

It can become discouraging when you see other people doing what it is that you want to do with your life. The internet makes this situation all the more obnoxious because people often fabricate how well they're doing in their lives with extreme exaggeration. It creates a psychological obsession for an onlooker to feel like they're just not good enough. It makes a speculator bitter when seeing someone that they went to school with, grew up with, etc., doing what it is that they want to do with their lives. Do we chalk it up to luck of the draw or justify it with not being good enough?

One cannot help the circumstances that they were born into but they can most definitely change them if they have the courage to. The biggest set up for failure for someone that was born into less than fortunate circumstances is not knowing that it doesn't have to be permanent. It takes a ton of courage and patience; something many people lack due to ignorance. When someone isn't aware of the many opportunities and resources available to them they become complacent and remain stuck in the circumstances that they're born into thus adding more to the circumstance and the cycle continues for the next generation.

Many of us could have gotten a lot further in life had we realized that everything wasn't as bad as it seemed at an early age. If we'd known when to rebel and fight for what we believed in, we could have gotten further. We can play the blame game all day long but at some point we must take responsibility over our own lives by educating ourselves on the many subjects of the world. You can claim to have all the book smarts or all the street smarts but you'll still fall short because one cannot be everywhere at once therefore there will always be a gray area that you're unfamiliar with. A person that claims to be content with street smarts will never know as much as they should.

They'll only know what's going on in their surrounding neighborhoods but will neglect to stay informed on what's going on in the rest of the world.

The fact is, life can be overwhelming because of the unpredictable curveballs that get thrown our way. It's easy to become depressed with our own situations especially when we think everyone else is doing better than us. I blame the internet. We live in the era of "real time". Not only is everything that we do in "real time" but everything we post online is in real time too…or at least that's what we try to portray. Social media gives life to the world of make-believe.

We're able to log onto our Facebook, Instagram, or Twitter accounts and become whomever we want to be. Many take advantage of this while the rest of us sit and watch with looks and feelings of annoyance especially when you personally know the individual. Some of us buy into the façade and really start to believe that the grass truly is greener on the other side and that we're the only ones facing difficult times.

Remember this: People will reveal to you only what they want you to see and know. There are some that only post negative things on their social media accounts putting everyone under the impression that they're really going through a lot when in fact it's not as bad as it seems. People are attracted to social media because it attracts attention and it creates a spotlight for them. Whether they're looking to play the victim or portray their life in a way that is not accurate, people have realized that they can create the image they want to sell via social media.

Social media, when used incorrectly, is poisonous to society. Narcissism is at an all-time high with this generation and you have the internet to thank for that. Everyone

wants to think it's about them and that they're starring in their very own reality TV show. I've decided to eliminate all of my personal social media accounts except Facebook. If it's not for business then I don't want to partake in it.

It creates unnecessary drama and makes the average person over obsess about what the next person is doing at every moment. It can drive you crazy if you let it. I say instead of spreading negativity, why not use the internet to spread positivity? Ever since I adopted the mantra "positive vibes only" things have gone smoother for me in times of a crisis. When you invite negativity in your life, you essentially allow negative things to happen.

How?

It's because you expect them to happen. Have you ever heard someone saying, "It was put out into the universe," or speak of something called "Karma" ? Well, I believe in those things. I don't necessarily consider myself to be a superstitious person but I do tend to believe things as I see them happening. I will say as I've gotten older, I tend to believe none of what I hear and only half of what I see… thanks to the internet.

Growing up, I was taught to treat people how I want to be treated and think positive. On many occasions where I would think negatively about something before it happened, something bad happened. Looking back, I now realize that I was challenging the universe to ensure that it would. At twenty-five, I would never let the hypothetical question,

"Could things get any worse?" fly out of my mouth. Because that would be me challenging the universe and most likely they would.

I would challenge the universe a lot as a young girl and for a long time on the day-to-day basis I found myself asking, "Why Me?" Well, why not me? If it weren't for those obstacles, would I be the woman that I am today? There are situations that I look back on and now realize that they did not have to go down the way they did. It's all about moving forward and staying positive but you live and you learn.

I learned that it's not always as bad as it seems. Most times, I was just being dramatic.

Nowadays, when something happens and it frustrates me, I try to look at it from a different perspective. Although this has frustrated me, what is the benefit of this happening? Sometimes negative things happen for our own good. For example, I

would get flat tires often when I drove a 2002 Pontiac Grand Prix. I drove that car for five years. From graduating high school until after college graduation and into my first job out of college. During those times, I use to think like, "Damn, there is always something wrong with my car."

I've been stranded so many times I can't even count them on one hand. When I got my 2nd car, a 2002 Pontiac Grand Prix, already had high mileage but it was clean, looked cool and was paid off. My friends at the time loved riding in it because the sound system was awesome and the car was in pretty good shape. What I soon started to realize was cars don't just run on gas, despite the fact that my mom stayed on top on me as far as getting the routine maintenance done. Cars age just like people and, like people if taken care of properly, will last longer than we expect them to.

The Grand Prix was already six years old when I received it and I was the third owner. The first owner was a salesman who drove that car all over the United States and my mom was the second owner. By the time I received the car it already had over 100,000 miles on it. The fact that I was able to drive the car another five years before giving it up at the tender age of 11 (in car years) is a blessing. Yes, I had to invest money in it, but as my mom would tell me, "You have to take care of what takes care of you." As frustrated as I would get with my car, it sure did take me a lot of places. If it weren't for my discipline and a couple of wise mechanics (who changed my outlook when it came to cars) I may not have had that car that long. I had friends all around me getting new cars every year and some were paying car notes. Looking back, I would not have wanted to pay a car note in college. If I had, I probably would not have a degree right now or it would have taken me longer to get it. Priorities trump everything. Now that I pay a car note, I appreciate the experience so much more.

Remain Positive: Everything happens for a reason and what you go through helps you grow.

Karma is real. I've been both on the giving the receiving end. But isn't that how it works? With Karma, what you give is what you get and what you get is what you'll eventually give. It's a cycle that can be either negative or positive depending on how you play it. Don't get me wrong, I've done things that I'm not proud of and things that I knew I shouldn't have been doing.

I knew better but that didn't stop me from doing it. Just like a boomerang, Karma would eventually come back to bite me in the behind. It never failed. The funny thing is when it happened, most times I knew why. I think when you're younger, you think certain things can't and won't happen to you but they can and they will. No one is exempt.

On the other hand, many times we can do everything right and then something unfavorable happens and we can't figure out why. I'm a firm believer in divine intervention. I believe that everything happens for a reason. It may not be something that we'll figure out or understand in that moment but hopefully, one day you'll have that aha moment and it'll all click for you. I've

been having these often over the past few years and many of the things that didn't make sense when I was going through them make sense now. There is always a reason.

To reiterate the effects of Karma: sometimes we don't realize that we bring certain things upon ourselves. There are certain things that happen to us that are happening because of a decision we made in the past. Do you disagree with that? There are people that we've wronged and went about living our lives like nothing happened, meanwhile leaving that person to suffer only for us to experience the same exact feeling later on. We wonder "Why?" without taking accountability. In the case where you may be the person that was

wronged, depending on how you chose to react, Karma typically will take care of it. I'm the type of person who usually let's the Universe deal the deck. I do believe in Karma and I've been lucky enough to see it get people together that I feel have wronged me. It doesn't necessarily make me feel good to see people suffer but I feel it is justice being served as many times people don't realize the effects of their actions until it happens to them. It's the only way we can learn sometimes.

Many times, when things go wrong, I try to figure out where it is that I went wrong. It is my belief of divine intervention that makes me look at things from this perspective. When did I stray off the path of God's plan for me? It's what I consider being accountable for my actions. The idea of cause and effect is often what gets us to the places we end up.

You cheat on someone, you're going to get cheated on. You do right by people, you will be blessed in other ways. Take a look around. What do you have that you consider a blessing? I'm sure there's at least one thing that you can show gratitude for. It's all because of good Karma.

All in all, be considerate of others and just be a good person. You can't go wrong with that. Positive vibes beat negative vibes any day. I weighed the Pros and Cons for you below and although there is so much more to gain from being optimistic. I've provided some suggestions below to help you remember why it's important to start adopting positive habits in your life. It's not a cookie-cutter concept.It starts with you and your daily habits. You can turn your life around just by keeping the list below in mind.

Positive Vibes

- Promotes energy
- Mood booster
- Good Karma
- Attracts good people in your life

Negative Vibes

- Sucks energy from body
- Promotes negative thoughts and depression
- Bad Karma
- Attracts people with poor intentions in your life

So, I want to focus back on Social Media and apply the concepts that we just talked about to that. I often see people expressing themselves via Social Media, and I get it. People feel like they should be able to say what they want to say on their accounts and no one should have anything to say about it. What people fail to realize is

negativity attracts negativity. If I were to make a status about how much my life sucks everyday, it

wouldn't make me feel better and it'll just be a constant reminder of how much I think my life sucks every time I go to log on.

Eventually, someone will feel the need to comment. They'll either say something in hopes of making you feel better or will try to counteract your negativity with another negative comment and you'll blow up and start going back and forth with that person. What I'm saying is why put that much energy into proving a point? A point that does not benefit you whatsoever.

Instead of getting on the internet to speculate everyone else's lives while comparing your life to someone else's who you assume is living stress free, choose to read between the lines. Everyone stresses about something at some point or another including myself. The thing is, everyone handles stress differently.

My advice: When life gets you down, the last place you should be looking for comfort is Social Media. Instead, surf the web and figure out a way to solve what ever problem it is that has you down. Do something about it. Venting via Social media every time something goes wrong in your life is not going to fix a thing. No one is going to come out of the wood-works and offer you a million dollars to fix your problems. Well, at some point someone will but most likely it'll be a scam and that'll just add more problems to your life. All in all, if you can't find a solution to your problems via the internet then I suggest you log off.

Turn the computer off and talk to God. That's always going to be my answer to everything, TALK TO GOD. Pray about it and figure out what it is that you need to change in yourself to make your life better because it starts with you and you're thinking process. Don't get swept up in the hype of the internet and social media to define who your are. Figure that out on your own when you're off the grid and actually living your life outside of the internet.

I want you to practice enjoying your life and being grateful for the things that you have. Set goals and achieve them to obtain things that you do not have but feel that you deserve. I'm here to tell you that hard work pays off. I'm a living testimony.

Everything that I'm talking about here I've done, and I had to learn that it's not the way to go about things. Speak positive things into existence and it shall happen but same goes for the negative things.

Choose wisely. What approach will you take in life. If I can just ask one favor of you—choose happiness EVERY DAY. Don't be blinded by what you see. Figure out what's really important to you and how that plays into your happiness and go for it. Life is short and you only get one shot. The internet and media have skewed our perception of reality.

Live everyday like it's your last and be the best YOU can be. God created you for a reason and it was not to duplicate yourself in the likes of anyone else but HIM. It is not of your concern to be just like the girl with 20k followers on Instagram or the

Guy with 100k followers on Twitter. God made you for a specific purpose. It is your job to figure out what that purpose is. It's ok to log off and simply live sometimes. You'll lose a lot of time being logged in. YOU CAN DO IT!

I've decided to close this chapter out with an incident that just happened on social media just now. One of my followers posted a video of a local female rapper talking down on educated people with degrees.

She said, *" What you gone do with a degree? Get a job? Whooo, I don't give a fuck. I can be a stripper like I was ..bitch making money. I made 26k in one night. I don't*

have to have a mother-fucking degree to have a mother-fucking job. Bitch, catch up mustards. "

Of course I felt the need to repost the video via the Repost Wiz app before it was told to me by the artist herself that, " It was meant for comedy," before ending the the comment with "Gosh". It was highly offensive to me as this isn't the first time that I've seen someone on the internet downplaying those that chose to stay in school. It's definitely an intimidation thing and it's so easy to flip it on the person that has something that you want. I can't think of any other reason why you would be mad. This particular post consistently raked in comments and likes for the next four hours.

It took me a good hour and a half before the internet got a response out of me. I wasn't going to comment at all. I've never had any of my inspirational posts

celebrating business owners, those climbing the corporate ladder and those who chose to be educators get as much attention on those posts as this. I'm sitting here like, how is it that this up and coming rapper is getting all this attention? It's because America is obsessed with glitz, glamour and fame.

I shared this video to my Facebook, which is the only personal social media account that I have and you'd be amazed at how many people had interacted with the rapper in real life and did not have nice things to say about her. I remember when I first noticed her, I was giving her props in a conversation with a guy I use to date. He said, "I know her from back in the day and you're nothing like her." In a sense he was

saying, "Don't be fooled by the glitz and glamour. She had to go through some things to get there."

Essentially, it's the same reason why many of her fans love her. However, if she could not benefit off of the fan base (monetarily) I'm sure people would see that other side to her much often. I have friends that have lived similar lifestyles as she and even they say, "The money was good but I wouldn't do it again." What I want to say is EVERYONE has a past but it's what you make of your future that matters. EVERYONE has a story.

We must humble ourselves and remember that one person is not better than the next. We must take a stand for what we believe in. I felt as though the video was a form of bullying and when I responded to it, it was flipped on me as being the aggressor. I suppose promoting a legit life is the wrong thing to publicize in today's world. I would have felt the same way whether I knew it was a joke or not and that's real.

It amazes me. What I want to leave you with is that it's all perception. You can't idolize everything you see on the internet because most of it is fluff and the only true idol is GOD. I want to inspire people, not for them to idolize me but to motivate them to be the best version of themselves. You see the difference?

What I want you to take away from this chapter:

- The internet can be used for both good and evil and sometimes the bad outweighs the good. If ever you log on and you're seeing things that invoke negative feelings into your atmosphere, log off. It's ok to go off the grid sometimes

- Be sure that you're contributing the GOOD to society via your social media channels. It's a power tool that can connect you to any and everyone here on earth. How will you impact society with your message?

Chapter 2

Tapping into your Intuition

My intuition was always there. I'm a woman. It showed up a few times before in my life before it decided it was there to stay at age 23. It's the reason why I write under the pen name, Intuitive Mimi. I've always believed I had a sixth sense when it comes to feeling things but I wasn't always sure how to channel that.

I've always heard that women have a "woman's intuition" and what I've learned as I got older is that men don't believe it. They think we're crazy to believe we have to psychic ability to not physically be somewhere when something happens but to feel that we know the truth about what happened. It's hard to explain but it's real. Looking back, I now realize that it's always been there. It's that gut feeling that tells you something isn't right.

It makes your nerves bad. The feeling doesn't go away either. Typically, if you ignore the first signs your body will continue to try to warn you in a series of events. Mine usually starts with a weird vibe. Next, there are specific thoughts that cloud your mind and you can't figure out why you keep thinking of the same thing over and over whether it's something that's happened in real life or not.

After that, the dreams usually follow. You start to see things in your dreams that translate to visions. If you ignore that, the bad vibes accompanied by nervousness follow, thus leading to that final gut feeling where you become pretty positive that something is not right. I believe there are many times where I've dodged situations because of weird vibes and it probably saved my life. However, there are times when I ignored the signs and had to face the repercussions. I knew better but wanted to be hard-headed.

I would look back on certain situations and think, "I knew, but why did I still do it?" Why did I go along with it? You live and you learn though. The signs are always there, but are you aware? I feel like you have to reach a certain level of wisdom in your life before you can really channel this gift and I don't believe it's a gift given only to women.

It's all about how in-tune you are with yourself. My mom use to tell me about dreams that she had where she felt as though they were visions or warnings and she predicted that it'd probably pass down to me. I didn't realize that this was a real thing until 2006 when I was sixteen years old and dating an eighteen year old who was fresh out of juvenile.

Now, I knew that he probably wasn't the guy for me and I probably talked to him over the phone for like a month before I decided to finally hang out with him, as we called it. We dated for a full three months after initially hanging out.

I met his friends and family. He took me on my first date to the movies and we spent a lot of time together. He was the perfect gentlemen. What I, slowly but surely, found was that he was controlling, abusive, and a cheater. Now, thank God I got out of the relationship in the nick of time before the abuse would start but we

had an incident right before we broke up that opened my eyes to the fact that he really had issues. It only took that one incident though.

After that, I would eventually come to find out that he was cheating on me anyway. As far as the abuse, the signs were always there. He just hid them in his controlling ways. I was lucky enough to end it at cheating because a mutual friend of mine later

told me how horribly he started to treat his girlfriend after me. It was full fledged domestic violence.

How I came to find out he was cheating was when I first noticed a change in behavior. It always starts there. He became rather distant. I didn't think much of it because we were around each other all the time, like everyday. So, I figured some time apart was good.

Of course, he still wanted to know my every move but that was the norm with him, no big deal. When I was around him, he was acting weird. This prompts my curiosity every time. I start looking for more clues but I didn't do that until I started having the dreams. I kept having a dream that I was going to break a nail and then we would break up.

I had that dream for like a good two weeks straight. At the time, I had long acrylic nails so it was likely that I would break a nail eventually. We had started arguing a lot so that tipped me off to start paying close attention to what was going on around me. One day, while we were hanging out over his house, I had the opportunity to look at his phone when he went to the bathroom. My number was not in the phone but someone else was saved under "wifey"...evidence!

I did not see him after that for maybe a week and the next time I saw him would be the night of the incident. My girls and I (friends at the time) were hanging out at one of his homeboys' house and he found out I was there. He came there from a party and was drunk. We were mad at each other because we recently had an argument and I was still feeling some type of way about what I found in the phone. He asked me to join him in his friend's basement so we could talk.

I joined him in the basement as my friends had ducked off somewhere. Typical teenage boy, he expected us to just makeup, or what you would call kiss and make up. My best friend and her best friend at the time came downstairs shortly after we'd had a talk where he basically fed me bullshit. My best friend knew better though and she had every intention on running interference. He never cared for her so this spiraled out of control very quickly.

My boyfriend at the time told my best friend to go upstairs and she said,"No we're not leaving unless she comes with us. His response was that I wasn't going anywhere. My friend's response was, "She is if she wants a ride home." I silently watched all of

this take place and then I started to gather my things as it was getting close to my curfew anyhow. Also, I could tell that my boyfriend was getting belligerent and I was absolutely turned off by his attitude. So, as I started to walk away from him and my friends started up the stairs, I suddenly fell backwards onto the couch behind me. I soon realized that he yanked me back by my hair.

He had a pretty tight grip on me. My two friends turned around to see what the commotion was about and quickly ran to my rescue. One of the girls demanded he let me go and he said to them, "I told ya'll to go upstairs and leave us alone." My best friend spoke up and said, "Oh hell naw, we're not leaving her down here with you." I could tell that her presence was further making him agitated and due to the headache that I was starting to get because he was still holding me down by my hair, I insisted to my best friend to go upstairs and that I'd be all right.

In that moment, I really believed I would be ok. I did not want to involve anyone else in my mess. I bravely told her to leave me with the psychotic drunk teenager convincing myself that I'd manage him fine by myself. The bible says to "walk by faith and not by sight." My two friends hesitantly headed up the stairs but not before telling me to yell if I needed them. In an instance, his friend yelled down to us that we had to get out of the basement because his mom had just pulled up.

Talk about saved by the bell. I had many moments like this, close encounters in my life where it must have been God that saved me in the brief moment where everything could have gone terrible wrong. I truly believe that God won't put more on you than you can handle simply because I've been involved in unfavorable events, mostly surrounding guys, but there wasn't one situation that I was not able to bounce back from. I would think to myself , "Why me?" Now I look back and ask, "Well why not me?" Every single struggle that I've experienced made me stronger. I would not be the woman that I am today had I not gone through some of the things I've been through. I was unhappy when I was going through those events.

I could tell you of many regrets during those phases in my life but I understand now and I no longer have any regrets. If I had to go through all that to get here, then it was worth it. After that particular night, I probably didn't see my boyfriend for an entire week. He did apologize to me and my friends before we left. Conveniently, my best friend stayed the night over there that night because she was having issues with her

mom and could not go home. She went back after dropping everyone off because I guess she felt like she didn't have anywhere else to go.

I thought nothing of it and even saw my boyfriend the next morning as he asked my friend to bring me to see him. It was after that morning in particular that I didn't see him for a week. Again, I thought nothing of it and a week later my best friend calls me to see what I was doing for the day. She also asked me had I talked to my boyfriend in which I replied nonchalantly, "Yeah." She then asked had I seen him recently. "I replied,"No."

Lastly, she invited me to the mall with her and her best friend and I quickly obliged before hanging up. Now, as I was hanging up, I started to close the window in the living room. It was super windy outside and the wind was blowing things around in the living room. Just as I got the window all the way closed, my nail broke. Sign #1.

The Mall…

We walked around the mall looking for an outfit with matching shoes for my friend. She had just gotten paid so like most teenagers, she wanted to go shopping with her hard earned cash. After about an hour or so, we decided to sit down to grab a bite to eat from the mall food court. During this time, my friend decided this

was the perfect moment to tell me that the guy that I claimed as my boyfriend had another girlfriend. She admitted to witnessing the proof a week ago and although he asked her not to tell me, she knew she would but didn't know how.

Her friend then spoke up and said, "I told her to just tell you while she was sitting around asking everyone else for advice." At the moment, I was not thinking about the fact that my best friend waited a week to tell me and even took me to see him the

next morning after it happened. I was thinking about how bamboozled I felt for getting into a relationship with a guy who would then later have me looking like a fool. I started crying right there in front of everyone in the food court and even though I disliked crying in front of people, it didn't matter because all I felt was hurt and anger. He was first on the list of guys that would make me cry.

I was just a few months shy of seventeen. In comparison to my friends, I guess I could be considered a late bloomer because of this. I'd seen plenty of my friends

crying over guys numerous of times since hitting puberty. Yet, here I was almost seventeen and it was just now happening to me. It happens to the best of us. It took me over a year to get over the betrayal.

Until this day, it still boggles my mind that someone that I spent so much time with still had enough time to cheat on me with someone else.

It's like —when did he sleep? There were other incidences after this in which I ignored my gut feeling but I wouldn't find out how strong my intuition really was until age twenty-three when I was in a relationship with who I refer to as #3 in a later chapter. The drama started just as I was getting ready to graduate from college. I had been in a relationship (or what I thought was a relationship) with a guy for almost two years before I found out that he had a child with someone else. He'd recently found out that he'd fathered a child five years prior.

He attempted to hide it from me as well as his secret relationship that he'd recently started to carry on with the child's mother. Let me tell you, it was the craziest piece of drama that I'd ever been involved in to date. Nothing tops what I went through during that break up. My nerves were so bad and I even lost weight because the man that I was in love with couldn't and wouldn't tell me the truth. I knew the truth though.

My intuition knew. I knew from the very beginning that he wasn't someone I should have gotten involved with. It seems like from the moment I told him, "You couldn't be my boyfriend." He took it as a personal challenge to get me and only to later prove my point as to why he should have never gotten chosen in the first place. From the very beginning, I knew but at the same time, I felt there was something different about him from the others.

He was persistent which in my eyes at the time meant he was genuinely interested. We met at the beginning of 2011 and started dating just a few months later, when he claimed to had caught feelings for me. It was all game. What I came to realize later is that sometimes persistence means nothing. Sometimes, men just like the chase.

He was persistent but kept an air of mystery about him. I would later come to find out that it wasn't mystery but rather him hiding things about himself, that he did not want me to know about. For almost two years, my

intuition remained in inactive mode. Up until then, I had to rely on my common sense. I had never suspected anything out of the ordinary about him up until the moment I'd saw him hugged up with another woman on Twitter with the caption, "Me and My Future".

Now I can't quite remember what prompted me to go on the woman's page except that I started to notice that she was commenting on his posts and liking them frequently. Now at this moment, we had already broken up as I felt like our relationship has run its course. I could also tell that he just wasn't invested in it as much as he should have been and I honestly felt like I could do better. Boy, do I wish I would have left it there. What should have been a quick and easy break-up became a long drawn out six months of dramatic events in which I would find out that the woman he was in the photo with was actually the mother of his child.

Apparently at the time that the photo was taken, he did not know that. Once he found out, that's when shit really started to hit the fan. My intuition was in overload. He tried his hardest to keep the truth away from me but the woman would be the one to tell me the truth. That is always a no-no when you're in a relationship with someone.

Prior to the DNA test results coming about, we had gotten back together. As a matter of fact, we weren't even broken up a full month before we got back together. Once she saw that, she tried everything in her power to break us up and when I say everything, I mean EVERYTHING.

The paternity test was just the icing on the cake. I'm not going to go back into the entire story because that's not what I want to focus on. Plus, it'll probably make me feel some type of way to re-visit a very unhappy time in my life when it came to that relationship. What I want to focus on within that particular event is what permanently activated my intuition. I believe it's always been there but this event was the moment when I learned to tap into it on-demand.

I saw things before they even happened and maybe some while they were happening. I saw things in my sleep. I would sometimes zone out in the middle of doing something. It consumed me. I have never felt such a high level of distraction over something that bothered me. It was because it bothered me that I would continue to seek answers.

Once I learned how to tap into my intuition on demand, it became more evident when someone was lying to me. I could hardly tell before and I would always give people the benefit of the doubt but now I know better. It was the series of events that followed me stumbling across that photo. It was the series of events that followed after and for the remainder of that year. Even when I moved on, the mess tried to follow me but I knew how to block it. I tried to move on because I learned during that break up that my ex was none of who he claimed to be.

Honestly, I took that hard. It was the hardest thing I ever had to go through in life and I could probably write an entire book on that experience alone. He would tell me one thing and I would get this sickening feeling in my gut. During this time I even started to hear from God more. He'd tell me to just leave the situation where it was; He's no good for you.

Being young, hard-headed, and in love, I didn't want to listen. So I had to go through the biggest heartache of my life because I didn't want to leave the situation when I was told to. I kept ignoring the warnings from my intuition and even allowed the situation to bring an ugliness out in me. Looking back, I can't even believe I allowed someone to take me out of character. I remember at one point feeling sorry for myself, thinking, "How the hell did I get into this situation?"

I tried to push the visions I saw in my dream to the back of my mind. I knew things that I should not have known because I wasn't physically there when they were happening but it was like I was there. Until this day, my ex can't figure out how I know some of the things that I know and is probably convinced that someone showed me but it was my intuition and GOD. You may think I'm crazy but your intuition is real and it lives inside of you. Use it and listen to it.

It'll save you plenty of wasted time. The scenario I just shared with you happened in 2013, so when my ex propositioned me at the beginning of 2015 to "try to work on us," although I agreed, I knew better. We'd been hanging out here and there five months prior to the proposition so I agreed because I wanted to see if he was serious. I am a believer of true love. As I've grown and matured, I've also realized that you're going to go through things with your loved ones and I figured, maybe we had to go through all that stuff to get here today.

We were honestly in a great place and I agreed with his proposition of, "Let's either work on being together in 2015 or stop hanging out all together." I understood his reasoning but he wasn't genuine about it. I'm not a fan of wasted time so why not work towards the greater? I wanted to see if he'd really changed like he claimed with the onset of age "30" hitting him. Now, I know better than anyone that no one changes overnight.

Once again, I wanted to give him the benefit of doubt. It gets me every time. In the back of my mind, I was skeptical because even though two years had passed since the drama I experienced with him, the messiness didn't stop when we broke up. We had separated two years ago and I was still trying to forgive him for all that had happened. I hadn't let it go. I didn't really trust him with my heart.

I still loved him but I didn't trust him. He'd lied to me about too much in the past. However, I thought it was pretty double standard for me to not have forgiven him but

to expect Jesus Christ to forgive me for all my sins so I went ahead and gave the relationship one last try. I would still keep an eye out though. As time went on, I started to grow hopeful.

I had to admit that I saw a change in him. I went from a "well, I hope it works out and if not, life goes on ," attitude to a perspective of "I understand that we had to go through some things but now we're in a great space and this is my husband." He initially took me to look at rings back in 2012 and in 2015 was telling me that he still wanted to get married and to me only. The good behavior lasted for a good two months before I was reminded that old habits die hard. I caught him in a few lies and then his behavior changed because of that.

My intuition screamed, " I TOLD YOU." It told me to get out now and to stay as far away as possible. I fought it for a few weeks, I'll admit. I just wanted him to communicate with me and once again he brought

out an ugliness in me that I never see except when dealing with him. He insisted that nothing was wrong and that I was just "trippin".

Once he saw that I was getting fed up again, he tried to flip it on me. We went through about three of these cycles before I decided to end it. I'm pretty sure that he was hiding something and his reaction to everything just proves that he was. But

again, I'm not going to go into detail about it, at least not in this chapter. Due to prior experiences with him, I was able to carelessly let him go for good.

The situation had gotten old and I knew better to begin with. No one has time to be on a merry-go-round with someone their whole lives. **Know your worth.** If someone is being dishonest with you, chances are their intentions aren't genuine anyway. Many times, people like that just want to feed off of your spirit and get whatever they can out of the situation before moving on to the next person.

Always remember, they'll be back. They always try to come back if they think they can but it's up to you to read between the lines. Rely on your intuition.

What I want you to take away from this chapter:

- It is important to dig deep within yourself so that you can become so in tune with your intuition that you're confident in your gut feeling.

- I want you to start out on a path of self discovery if you haven't done so already so that you can thrive more efficiently in this world. Read more books, get closer to GOD and find out your WHY.

- Once you find out your WHY, no one will be able to stop your elevation. Anytime someone tries to get in the way of your WHY, you'll run interference yourself rather than waiting on someone to rescue you.

Chapter 3

Never Let Your Left Hand Know What Your Right Hand Is Doing

The title of this chapter is a cliche that I've heard so many times while growing up. I never truly understood it until I became an adult. What I'll tell you is that this is something that's very hard for an expressive person to do. However, what I have learned is if you get in the habit of always broadcasting every single thing that you do or are going to do, then when will you ever have time to do it? You'll be too busy talking to realize that time has passed and you're still standing in the same spot while everyone else has moved on.

I cannot stress enough that knowing this and understanding this is essential to succeed in life. You may have a really great idea that you plan to implement but if you go around telling everyone what that plan is then there is a big chance someone may also think it's a great idea. Meanwhile, you're spreading the word telling everyone how you're going to do it, and one of those people will possibly go off and implement your great idea.

Ladies and Gentlemen, you just can't tell everyone EVERYTHING. For one, everyone isn't telling you everything about them. Believe that. For two, everyone doesn't have your best interest at heart.

You may feel like you really vibe with someone and they're trustworthy but I guarantee the minute you fall out with them, everything you've shared with them they've either already told other people (most likely) or will spread what you've told them to the world out of spite. What I've come to find is "the less people know about you, the better." It's the only way to protect yourself in a world where people come and go with no warning. Live by this: If it's something that you wouldn't want repeated, keep it to yourself.

Especially, when it comes to handling your business. Successful people move in silence. Unless the person is your business partner or loved one, inquiring minds do

not need to know. What I've come to find is when you're telling people your every move and anticipated moves they'll either try to mimic what you're doing and beat you to it or they'll try their best to distract you. Never forget: "they want to see you do good but never better than them." Believe that.

It amazes me how many friends I lost over the years as I continued to progress. Some of these people I thought I'd be friends with forever and then there were others who I knew their time would expire soon enough. It began when I started my college career. People I'd been friends with since elementary school and middle school were the first to go.

To be honest we started going down separate paths once I entered high school and the pressure became too much once I enrolled in college. From high school on up, I had started to make new friends and my old friends, I had started to realize, weren't really friends. They were what I'd call fair-weather friends. These are the type of people that only want to be bothered with you when there is nothing else in the world to do or when they're going through something. Other than that, you don't hear from them.

They always want you to be there for them but are nowhere to be found when you need them to be there for you. A person starts to pay attention to things like that as they get older. One thing about these type of people is that they always make sure to check in every now and again. Why? So you can update them on all things new since the last time you both spoke and so they'll have something to talk about later with their other friends. Don't be someone's entertainment unless that was your intention.

Keep your eyes open for these type of people. They almost always carry these type of characteristics. Graduating from college taught me plenty. It taught me things that I was not yet ready to accept but it was time to open my eyes.

Let's go back to 2008-2009, during my freshmen year of college. I did my first two years at a community college, mostly because I was mad that I could not go to an out-

of-state college due to funding. Also, I did not apply to any colleges back home because I didn't want to stay here. Time continued to pass and I realized that I would have to enroll in a school regardless, so I decided to do my first two years at a community college (to save money) and then I'd transfer to a university in time for my program. Smart, I know. :-)

I've found that people will see your brilliance. They'll see your light shining from within and thus try to pick your brain to see what it is that makes you tick so they can then apply it to their life and pass it off as a genuine part of their personality. Be

aware of these type of people.They'll try to steal your ideas and pass them off as their own. They'll try to find out your timeline and beat it because to most, it's a competition. I do not exaggerate but remember, the original is always better that the copy...ALWAYS. They can duplicate your ideas but not your passion for it. Move in silence as best you can!

I want to give you a glimpse of the type of environment that I grew up in. Some could say the odds were definitely stacked against me but I was always determined not to become a product of my environment. As I reflect on my life, I don't think people believed I would actually graduate from college with a bachelor's degree. I was raised by a single mother due to my biological father struggling with a heroine addiction for all of my life.

I was not as privileged as some of my classmates but I recognized that I was still more privileged than many others that I'd come into contact with throughout my life. My dad's side of the family had a mixture of different types of people. Some led successful careers, while others didn't. However, I did not come in contact with some of these family members on the regular, if even at all. Regardless of whether or not

some of my family members on my dad's side were educated, many were doing pretty well for themselves.

My mother's side of the family is a completely different story. I've seen struggle on both sides of my family but my mom's side of the family is full of single mothers. In fact, my mom is the only one in her generation (in her immediate family) besides my grandmother to marry. I was the first person on my mom's side of the family to graduate from college with a bachelor's degree. My mother has an associate's degree in Business Administration, so naturally I would adopt her "business woman" mindset.

Many of the men in our family didn't go to college and most don't even have high school diplomas. It was just easier to be in the streets, I suppose. I am a hardworking woman from Highland Park, MI. HP was a city once known for its beautiful trees but now known for it's notorious drug problem. It is a city where addicts walk the streets and it's the norm but it wasn't always that way. In fact, I remember Highland Park, or

HP as most call it, being such a beautiful city. I remember this and cherish the memory fondly as things started to change for the worst as we got older.

I remember when some of the burned out houses and buildings were actually places where people use to dwell and live. I can only imagine how it looked while my mom was growing up. Many don't realize that Highland Park is a suburb of Detroit and just like Detroit, there are still some nice parts. It's all about how you take care of your property.

When we weren't in Highland Park, we were on the westside of Detroit at a relative's house, running freely amongst the other kids. Usually, it was because my mother was either at work or had adult plans so we'd stay there until she returned. I remember my cousins being in gangs, drinking forties at an early age and smoking cigarettes. You had young girls sexually active as early as twelve years old and having babies by the tender age of sixteen.

My mom would always tell me these crazy unfortunate stories about people that she knew and how since the particular incident, their lives weren't the same. My mom

was the type of mom that didn't trust anyone and I could understand why but I really didn't comprehend the WHYs until I became an adult. It wasn't as much about trusting no one as it was about not putting anything past anyone, even those we decide to trust. Even in church, they talk about not putting your faith in man kind but rather in God and I understand why. I'll use this moment to drive us back to the main point of this chapter.

"Never let your left hand know what your right hand is doing!" My mom has told me this so many times growing up. Simply put, everyone doesn't need to know everything about you. I've always thought of my self as an open book meaning I considered myself as genuine as it gets.

If someone wanted to know something about me then all they had to do was ask. I'm an honest person who keeps it real so in the past it was no big deal for me to tell someone something so personal about me especially if I feel like I really vibe with them.

What I've learned from doing that is most people are not going to tell you everything about them or everything that's going on with them. So why should I tell anyone EVERYTHING about me? I think one of the most disappointing things that I've ever

experienced in life is being so open with people that were hiding things from me. I will say, however, that it taught me an obvious lesson.

"Everyone doesn't need to know EVERYTHING and never let your left hand know what your right hand is doing." If for any other reason, let that be the reason.

Beyonce did it best!

"Changed the whole world when that digital dropped!" -Beyonce, Feeling Myself (remix)

Beyonce dropped an entire digital-only album at the end of 2013 that had the internet going crazy and left the Bey Hive not knowing how to act. Her most loyal fans were both ecstatic but also disappointed because they had no idea that the album would come out so soon. They expected that Beyonce would keep her loyal fans in the loop, but it's not always about that. Sometimes, it's merely about staying FOCUSED. Beyonce was already being bugged about when it was that she would release another album and probably didn't want to be bothered with the stress of a public deadline.

The pressure of knowing that everyone expects you to do this BIG thing and on the world's deadline can be overwhelming to say the least. Sometimes the best way to get things done is to stay out of the way and fly under the radar for a while. I know. I've been there and it's worked for me in the past; that's why I never take it personal if I don't hear from someone for a while because I GET IT. You have to take some time to yourself to get things in order and that's exactly where I am (again) at this point in my life.

2015

I quit my job today. No, I don't have another job lined up and only three people know by default. Only one is a relative. I've been thinking about doing this for a while. I was not happy at my place of employment (hence the introduction to this book) and I feel that there is a company out here that I can grow within and they'll pay me what I'm worth as a degree-holder.

Meanwhile, I recently started my own business and that's been my primary focus outside of having a day job. Now, obviously my business is not making enough money as to where I'm able to live off of it alone. So, yes, I will be looking for another job and I have faith that I'll find one soon. I decided that I don't want anyone (besides the three that already know) to know that I'm unemployed right now. Why? Because it'll prompt curiosity. It'll prompt questions and negative responses.

"Why would you quit your job without having another one lined up?"

At this point in my life, I cannot afford to house negative vibes or mindsets. I am absolutely thinking positive about the current transition that is happening in my life. Negative feedback will distract me. It'll take me off my focus. It'll have me worrying about things that I don't have time to worry about.

So, right now, I'm choosing to fly under the radar and let people think that I'm still working a nine to five. It'll prevent people from calling me during traditional work hours and I'll be able to stay focused and work on what I need to work on. It makes the most sense when trying to stay focused on the goal.

What I want you to take away from this chapter:

- Everyone doesn't need to know EVERYTHING about you, what you're doing at every moment, and what you're planning to do.

- It's not conducive to your success and it's just not productive for you. The things I've shared with you in this chapter about my upbringing, many do not know. It's because as I got older I realized, "It doesn't matter where I came from or where I've been." You should think of life's journey the same.

- What matters most is where you're going. People will speculate anyhow. Most probably wouldn't guess some of the things I revealed about myself. In fact, most people that I've met more so recently pre-assume that I grew up in a two parent home and that my parents were married. False. My parents were engaged, yes, but never married and for the last 11 years of my life I lived in a two parent home which isn't half bad but what does that really mean? I know people whose parents

- were married their whole lives and they turned out worse off than I did. Ignore labels.

Food for thought: "Never Judge A Book By Its Cover."

Chapter 4

You Get What You Focus On, So Focus On What You Want

FOCUS. What does that word mean to you? *Dictionary.com* has 10 definitions for this one word. The first being: A central point, as of attraction, attention or activity. Basically, what you give attention to is what you'll get. As in drama, relationships, positive thoughts or negative thoughts just to name a few. We tend to give attention to what we're attracted to. For example, those attracted to drama always seem to be in the middle of some sort of conflict.

If this is not what you're trying to be around then I'd avoid those type of people. Me personally, as outspoken as I am, I dislike confrontation. I don't like having to say something to someone about something unfavorable that they did. However, sometimes it has to be done.

I tend to try to avoid drama. I'm all about paying attention to vibes and wish to only immerse myself in positive ones. I try not to breathe life into negative thoughts and always try to keep the bigger picture in mind. Nothing bad ever came from being

focused as long as you're focusing on something productive. The mantra is true to its meaning and I have examples from both sides.

Obvious fact: I'm a female. As long as I can remember, I've always known that I was to be attracted to the male species and so having a significant other was genetically implanted into my DNA before I was even thought of. I always knew even as a little girl that this was the norm and I was to follow it. It meant I was normal if I had a boyfriend and that was what I focused on aside from everything else. I focused on having a boyfriend, boo, hubby, bae, whatever the kids are calling it these days and focused on that alone.

Being able to give that title to someone meant that I was doing exactly what society expected of me as a female. I must keep a "boo" to align myself with the norm. It was essential to fit it in. What society doesn't teach you is there is so much more that goes into it. Once you get past the title you must continue to build on that foundation.

That's assuming that you started building a foundation before throwing a title on it. See, where I messed up was not fully understanding how relationships work. I focused on the title and that's all I ever really got. I was focused on the wrong thing to say the least. People say, "A bond is better than a title," and I agree with that to a certain extent. I say you need both.

You need to build a relationship on a foundation and that's where bonding comes into play. You must spend time with each other! This formula goes for familial, friendship and romantic relationships. Arriving at an understanding of what's to be expected of each party in the relationship is where the importance of a title comes into play. For example, if I work for a company where my title is a Manager then off rip, people will know that my position comes with more power than say someone who's just a regular employee.

They'll tend to not do certain things around me and will hold a certain level of respect for me in comparison to their other co-workers. It's one of the laws of nature. Relationships are also important when it comes to

this scenario. If you're a super laid back manager and allow your employees free-reign then when it's time for you to enforce policies, your employees may not take you seriously; there goes that foundation. You get what you focus on.

If you're more concerned with everyone liking you on your job than actually doing your job, then you'll be left either demoted or jobless with a lot of "friends" who most likely wouldn't look out for you more than you've looked out for them. Life is all about adapting but that's a different lesson for another day. What I want you to take from that example is to stand up for what you believe in and follow your purpose.

You can't live for everyone else before you live for yourself.

In my relationships, I was pretty much content with a person giving me a title. I actually believed that the title would automatically keep both of us in check. Well, it kept me in check but often times the other person was still off doing what ever it was that they wanted to do. A title does not build a bond and it does not automatically bind you or the other person to the relationship. A title should not automatically grant a person benefits that they haven't worked for.

Looking back, I realized that guys saw that I was after a title and played right into it. I did not understand that just like school and work, relationships were work too. I often rewarded people with things they did not deserve (including myself) when all they

gave me was a title and a fantasy. I didn't really work for the title and they didn't work for me. It's all apart of being young and naive but luckily with experience you eventually learn (hopefully) and understand why certain situations turned out the way they did. I understand now.

My mom tried to talk to me about relationships as much as time allowed but often times, we have to go through things before we fully understand why it's being told to us. There were certain things that my mom told me that I didn't need to go through. Just hearing the horrible story was enough but then there were other things, things that seemed simple enough that I just didn't grasp until just recently. Looking back on my experiences as a teenager and the first half of my twenties, I've come to connect

the dots on things that my mother warned me about in regards to things that I've gone through in both friendships and romantic relationships. Mother knows best.

In my opinion, a person can't give you advice on something they've never experienced. Sometimes you'll have to just figure it out on your own. My first relationships that I've experienced in life were familial and then friendships outside of the household. Many of those relationships were short lived. Being raised by a

single mother, I didn't see my father much due to the lifestyle that he chose. There are times in my life where for a period of time, I would see him a lot and then he would disappear and I wouldn't see him for a long time.

I hate to say it but most, if not all, my relationships men have been this way. I like to believe that there are some women whom are not tremendously affected by their absentee fathers. In fact, many of my friends who grew up without fathers have loving relationships (or so it seems). I'm sure they struggle with some things but I can only speculate. I just happen to be affected in different ways than them. I will honestly admit that I'm aware that I have abandonment issues and it's something that I'm working on everyday.

It's the reason why I'm so against long distance relationships. I'm not sure what it was about a title that had me believing it would keep a person in my life. It had me thinking that their loyalty would be automatic. Maybe it has a lot to do with my relationship with my biological father. No matter how many times he left, I always knew I'd see him again.

Why? Because he's my father and I am a part of him. You can't leave a part of you behind permanently. You can take a break from it, but at some point you'll have to return to it. Although there was a part of me that was angry that he missed a lot of important moments in my life, it just kind of became the norm and it still is. The negative effect is that it also became the norm in my other relationships. It made me both an inpatient person altogether and too patient at the same time.

Let me explain:

Most of my relationships have lasted no longer than three months at a time. Why? Because I expect a lot from people. If I spend too much time with you, the relationship gets boring and predictable. Plus keep in mind, I'm not use to being around men (outside) of my family like that. This was the outcome for those that I just "liked" and more so rushed into things with. However, on the flip side, there have been a few men in my life that really captured my heart.

These were men that I'd met at places I had to frequent by default: work, church, school, etc. Some of those relationships took place over several years on and off and back to back. The short relationships took place during the "breaks" with these men. All three of the men (that'd capture my heart) had many things in common when it came to their personality and in one way or another possessed a similar personality trait that my dad also possessed. All three were absentee as well but in different ways.

All three constantly fed me excuses as to why they wanted to be around all the time but couldn't. The first relationship started when I was 13 (about the same age my mom and dad started dating) and ran its course by age 21. By then, I had met number 2 at age 17 and number 3 at age 21. He was two years older than me (same as my brother). I met number 1 at a church I was attending with my best friend at the time. I'd lived on the other side of town so naturally this was not a person I saw everyday. I mostly saw him on either Wednesday if my mom allowed me to go or Sundays when I went with my friend and we'd stay for both services.

Number 1: 2002

It's funny, I still remember what I had on the day we locked eyes for the first time. I had on a black with blue stitch quarter sleeve top with an American flag across the front. My pants were hip hugging jeans that I could rock because I was a skinny teenager and could pull it off. :-) My best friend had done the front of my hair in twists. I remember walking past him in the hallway to go into the sanctuary. Now, I'd already noticed him but that day would be the day that he'd finally notice me. He stopped me to inquire about who I was because he'd never seen me before.

I might have said something like "Oh, I'm here with my friend," who he then inquired about. Because it was after service, we had to get ready to head to the car. By then he started to follow me into the sanctuary and held the door for me while we locked eyes and smiled at each other. Eventually, he followed me to my friend's parent's car and gave me his number. We went on to talk on and off for the next few years and started officially "dating" my sophomore year of high school (three years later). He took me to homecoming and everything. He'd also be the same guy to eventually take my virginity.

I'd definitely consider the relationship to be "long distance". During our relationship, I lived east and he lived west. We talked on the phone a lot, which is normal for that age range. By this method, we learned a lot about each other but let's be honest, both he and I were talking to other people as well. Somehow we always found our way back to each other. This would go on for years before I'd officially move on for good. What made me give up on him? We had an awesome bond or so it seemed.

Everyone knew about him; it was apart of my package. What I'd eventually learn was he was a BOY. It came out later that a friend of mine at the time was secretly taking phone calls from him that were inappropriate (which only made both parties look bad). He consistently made false promises, plans for the future, etc.. It took forever for him to come through on just one of his promises.

Eventually, I wasn't really feeling the whole waiting around on him game. I was impatient when it came to that. I've never been a fan of waiting around on anyone and so I moved on to other people as teenage girls do. It later came out that he'd gotten someone pregnant in the midst of one of the times we decided to rekindle. I

wasn't really mad because we were never really together and by the time that had happened, I understood that.

It was simply puppy love and history that kept me liking him. Honestly, looking back, I think I just liked talking to him. I remember we'd be on the phone all night talking to each other. Even after his mom or my mom would try to make us get off the phone. One of us would sneak and call the other back. Those were the days.

I continued to run into him over the next few years but it was the same pattern every time and as you know, sometimes things just get old. He was also a habitual liar and a follower, so I became bored with him indefinitely. Nice guy, but he was never on my level of thinking. I don't really have any ill feelings against him because in a way, I was pretty aware of what I was dealing with. My dad had long prepared me for the inconsistencies, the lying, false promises, and cheating so I pretty much knew how to deal with the situation.

Looking back, I wouldn't say we were together. We just had history and I'm fine with that. I really liked him at a point in time but I was young, what did I know except he wasn't worth it. I knew that but still am glad he was the one I lost my virginity to. It could have been someone way worse. My friends have told me stories about their first time/first love and I'm completely fine with my choice. I want to point out that I was never formally introduced to his mother because this is an important fact of my history of relationships.

It's funny because whenever we'd link up, he always tried to pin the fact of our relationship not blossoming as it should to me having commitment issues. Why should I commit to a guy that I knew for a fact was talking, sleeping with, and claiming other girls? Of course, he's not going to own up to that. Now, numbers

two and three…I'm not sure what happened but it was nothing like number one. It was better, but then worse in a sense.

Number Two: 2007

I actually crown number two as my "first love." He was not my "first" but in a sense he was my first when it came to a lot of other things. I loved this guy's soul. We spent more time together than number one by default because he lived on the same side of town as me. I met him at my job that I was working at the time so I saw him a lot. When I say that first impressions last…it was proven in this situation. I remember the

first time I saw him, he was introduced as another employees boyfriend. I was kind of surprised because he didn't seem like her type but who am I to judge.

Note that the first time I saw him, he did not see me because he was working.

He didn't see me for the first time until about a few days to a week later. I remember coming down the stairs in the kitchen of the establishment and him saying something flirtatious to me and all I could do was roll my eyes and think, "he looks like a player." This was my reaction because I was told he was someone's boyfriend and I didn't understand why he'd flirt with me. This happened a few more times before I

mentioned it to my co-worker who happened to be the sister of the alleged "girlfriend". My co-worker informed me that they'd broken up a while ago due to her cheating on him and that her sister was just telling people that. Apparently, there was some truth to that. After finding that out, I then started being nicer to him.

He was cute after all so he at least deserved a break right? Especially with all that he's been through with his ex. That's so like me, to empathize with the other party. I didn't need to empathize with him. In fact, I owed him nothing. He kept trying to get my attention and eventually he did. I would soon agree to go on a date with him and I did. I remember it like it was yesterday. We went to see The Simpson's Movie.

I wore all white and curled my hair, which was a coppery brown at the time. We continued to go on dates for the next few weeks before finally hooking up. We spent so much time together that first month. It was crazy to me. I saw him like every other day and I wasn't use to that. He was four years older than me. I was impressed with the fact that he courted me as a man should.

He didn't like to talk on the phone much. He was more so of a "talk in person" type of guy. Looking back, that would bother me but knowing what I know now, that's not so bad. I remember staying up late into the night talking about everything: our goals,

our childhood, everything. Thinking about it still makes me feel some type of way to this day.

Perhaps there's a part of me that will always care, as it's said. I remember he used to let me let me drive his car so I'd have a way to work. My mom and I were sharing cars at that time. It was my senior year of high school and I didn't have my own car yet. So he'd let me drive his. I'd drop him off at work because he had to go in earlier than me. I'd leave for a few hours before returning to work myself. Ironically, I'd eventually ended up doing the same later on in our relationship once I got my car.

I didn't mind doing things for him because I always felt like he'd do it for me. I later find out that wasn't the case. I was constantly giving everything to this guy and

hardly getting anything in return. It was always about his benefit over everything else. I later learned that there was another side to him. He was very selfish and self-centered and didn't want to be around my people and hardly brought me around his.

Note: I was never introduced to his mother either. To this day, we have never met.

For example, when we went on dates and spent time together it was like our relationship was a secret. I'd come to learn this after it'd come out that he got another girl pregnant. Now, this happened while we were so called together but I didn't find out for sure until we broke up. I say that because it was mentioned to me but then never brought up again. He made it seem like it was just a theory and there was no way that he was the father and he never brought it up again. I'd find out from my mom, who also worked with us but by then I was no longer working there. I had moved on once I enrolled in college.

My intuition tried to warn me that something was up. I even saw text messages from the child's mother several months before this happened. He swore up and down that nothing was going on but then this happened. Why did this happen? Why was I exposed to this type of disappointment? He knew my mom would tell me and had the audacity to try to call me later that day to check on me. I went off of course and we didn't talk for probably about two months. This was when I started to receive private calls which I later found out was him. It was him calling to tell me how much he

missed me and how miserable his life was. So three months after the shocker, I started to come around again per his request.

Let me tell you, that was one of the hardest times of my life. Imagine trying to deal with the fact that the man you are in love with, all of a sudden, has a child with someone else. I met this young man with no children. Now, he had one and I still didn't have any; That's an adjustment. I'm sitting there trying to take in the baby carriage that now sat in his bedroom. A baby carriage that wasn't there before. He was feeling displaced and I could tell.

It was not only a lot to take in for me but for him as well. He wanted me to be his backbone in all of this but I couldn't. The year was 2009. I was a few months away

from turning twenty, and too young to be a step-mother. I remember him showing me photos of the baby (at the time) and I remember thinking, "She's cute," but the words wouldn't come out of my mouth. I just looked.

He sensed my silence as uneasiness and said, "I know this isn't easy for you but can you at least say something…like aww." I thought to myself, he has no idea what I'm feeling right now but typical of him to want me to disregard my own feelings. Is me being here not trying enough? Per usual, my feelings never seemed to matter when it comes to getting hurt. Everyone expects me to be strong because I'm such a strong person (so they speculate). EVERYONE has feelings. People don't realize when they make decisions, it affects everyone involved. This guy in particular always expected me to just roll with the punches.

As time went on, I came to realize what type of person he was. He always wanted others to feel sorry and sympathize with him, but he never considered how he made others feel. Though he claimed to understand or be sorry, he always found a way to turn it into something about him. It was always about what he was going

through. Makes you wonder, who was the man and who was the woman? It lasted about a good month and a half to two months before we'd end up having a big fall out.

This happened because he kept hopping back and forth between his child's mother and me. I remember feeling like someone stabbed me in the stomach and kept turning the knife during our blow up which took place over the course of two days. I remember crying on the living room floor. I'd never experienced hurt like this. I had

confronted him about her and him living together and it had turned out to be true. Just like that, right up under my nose…again.

Eventually, I figured it was time to move on. Hurtful words were exchanged between the two of us and I didn't talk to him again until the baby was about nine months old. That was about four to five months later. I just gave you the shell of our relationship now let me give you a detailed summary.

Back to the beginning of *Number Two* from 2007-2010 in grave detail

As stated before, I met my first love the month before my eighteenth birthday. Once I agreed to go on a date with him, we continued to go out on a few more dates and just hang out in general after that. He use to come over and go swimming in my apartment complex and I even spent my eighteenth birthday with him. He picked me up early in the morning, we went to breakfast and he got us a room in which we chilled heavily because it rained the whole day. Later on, we went to dinner and that was literally the only day he ever mentioned introducing me to his mom but I didn't want to meet her because I had been drinking.

Around month three of us talking, he told me he loved me while we were in the midst of an argument. He also talked me into buying him some Jordans for his birthday and two weeks after he retrieved them he hit me with a "I feel like we're drifting apart." You understand what just happened there right? He would never come over to

properly meet my mom. My mom requested to meet him outside of work and he wouldn't do it.

I continued to talk to him though because I saw potential in him. I was so young but felt entitled to experience what adults experienced because I was in a rush to grow up. I kept making excuses for him and it would only get worse before it got better.

I remember when we first started talking he would call me just seconds after I got out of his car to tell me he missed me. I remember trying that months later and he hit me with "Why? You just left." He was very wishy-washy all throughout our relationship. One minute he cared, the next he didn't. I was strung along in this very fashion for almost four years.

We enjoyed ourselves when we went out, rather it was the arcade, go-kart racing, movies, dinner, the park, etc..we did, for the most part, enjoy each other's company. After the Jordan debacle, we drifted apart as he called it. I actually started talking to another guy for a couple months. It wasn't until after I got my senior pictures back and my mom showed him my photos that we ended up having a conversation at

work. We continued to talk after that and I actually later spent my prom night with him as he bought me a Jacuzzi Suite

that night. I couldn't go to the actual dance with him because he was twenty-one at the time but we had a great night.

I remember we stayed up until 5:00am the next morning. It was definitely a night to remember as he professed his love to me. He told me he really loves me and gave me all the reasons why. It was super romantic to say the least. He said I always put a smile on his face when he sees me and that my personality keeps him wanting more. He claimed it was just hard to get serious about females because he doesn't trust them but he wanted me to know that he truly loved me (so he said).

Prom night gave birth to a feeling that I'd never felt before. My heart was on fire. I was beaming with so much love for this guy. The night of graduation (just a few weeks later), my friends and I went to the local arcade after my graduation dinner. He picked me up from there and I spent the night with him.

This was the night that I saw the texts from his child's mother. I had already gone through the text message scandal with a previous boyfriend so I was smarter this time…or so I thought. I looked in the outbox and saw him sending long-form text messages to a number that was not saved in his phone telling the girl that he loved her more than anything or anyone. I remember confronting him about it and he played stupid.

We talked about the situation again days later and I was told that I should know that I'm the only one for him, when he gets his "shit" together. That was a red flag right? I still bought into at the time. When he told me on prom night that he didn't trust females, it didn't resonate until after the fact. Looking back, it makes sense based on his stories about his mom. I've come to the conclusion that he has mommy issues and

the same can be said about number 1 and number 3. All three of these men had major situations that happened with their mothers in which their trust was betrayed.

He was not someone I should have moved forward with solely based on that fact alone. We continued to spend time together. Actually we spent plenty of time together after that. We'd get rooms so we could spend the night with each other because I lived with my mom and he was still living with his mom. We'd then ride to work with each other from the room. I just knew he loved me just by the way he held me at night. We talked for over a year before officially deciding to be in a relationship but it sure felt like we were together.

I guess what's understood doesn't have to be explained, huh? I remember spending the night at his mom's house numerous times over the year but was never introduced to her. It's funny when you look back on it and wonder how that was even possible.

At that moment in my life, he was the only guy that I'd ever talked to that long and consistently. Usually, I would have gotten bored or the person would have done something to turn me off. He was doing a lot of things that should have turned me off but didn't.

In my mind, there was something about him. During the entire span of our relationship there have been other guys here and there but I loved HIM. Looking back though, I'm not sure why. I think it was because of my experiences with him. I'd experienced many things with him that I hadn't with other guys but I was also young and had a ways to go. I wasn't as advanced as some of my friends were when it came to guys, so in comparison to them, I had a late start.

Sometimes I felt as though I loved him more than he loved me and he had two different personalities that I had to deal with regularly.

He was constantly apologizing for "what he put me through" but continued to put me through things. I remember feeling hurt when I didn't get anything for my birthday one year and the fact that I knew he was lying to me about the girl and the text messages. Come to think of it, he's never bought me a gift or done anything out of the way for me in which he did not benefit directly. There were times where he was super romantic but it was because he wanted something in return. That's what it was always about.

I remember being so pissed at times and thinking, "Why should I even continue talking to him?" I couldn't even think of a reason but I kept going back. Looking back, it was more so a physical attraction that kept me coming back more than anything. He sold me an illusion that I lusted after each and everyday. He had me thinking when he got his shit "together," We were going to be together.

I remember writing in my diary, during my first semester of college about the non-progression of our relationship while stating "next thing you know —he'll have a baby on the way," and exactly that happened six months after I called it. I was

questioning everything at that moment. I knew this guy could only lead me to disaster but I kept going back.

I left the job that we worked at together upon my first day of college so I figured anytime after that was a test of our relationship. I remember him giving me flowers for Sweetest Day when I came to pick him up to take him somewhere. It was the little surprises like that which kept me holding on just a little longer. He mentioned to me two months after starting my first semester of college that he may have twins on the way. After that, it was never brought up again.

I even brought it up and he just brushed it off saying, "I don't think I'm the father. There's a possibility that it's someone else's and she's not mentioned anything else to me." I even asked who the chick was and he said someone from a while ago and that's why he knows he's not the father because the timing doesn't add up. It never occurred to me that it was the text message girl. During this time, I was taking him back and forth to work.

Despite having to deal with his attitude and him snapping at me from time to time, I was still taking him to work and all he would give me was five dollars and that was if I was lucky. During that time gas was over four dollars a gallon and his job was more than twenty miles away, which was my car's miles per gallon. He lived several cities away from me, so to drive from where I lived, go to pick him up and drive a ways from where he lives to take him to work was a lot for just five dollars. Apparently, that's all he felt that I deserved.

Toward the end of my first semester of college, I asked him "Are we together...it's a yes or no answer." His response, " I thought you were fucking with someone else." Yet, he was constantly calling me to do him favors like take him to work and still sleeping with me any chance he got. This shows you how manipulative he was. It was because he was "fucking" with someone else.

He said, "It was never discussed before," as if he never sat in my face professing his love to me, talking about us being together, etc.. He had no issue with lying to my face but I kept going back. I kept feeding into

it. Almost a month after that conversation, he decided that we were together. The issue was, at nineteen this shouldn't have been a priority at all. I cared too much about having a man and being in love when school should have been my only focus.

We broke up two months after. I found out about his baby a month after we broke up. We didn't talk for about four months after that and then we got back cool in which he told me the truth about everything. At that point, I figured we'd never be together rather just remain friends.

I should have kept that mindset. Friends and friends only. He asked me if we could start over and I took the bait, of course. Later, we ended up falling out again the month before I turned 20 years old and we didn't talk or see each other for six months before he reached out to me… requesting to see me.

Eventually, I agreed to go to the movies with him the day before Valentine's Day of the following year even though I was technically dating someone else.

2010

Again, he asked if we could start over. We eventually started hanging out every week as I started seeing the guy I was actually dating less and less. Number two seemed like the guy I met initially. He was affectionate and often used terms of endearment when referring to me.

He'd say things like, "We're going to get married," but at this point I wasn't really interested in being more than friends because historically, he's known for having commitment problems. We were five months aways from year three of knowing each other. I remember my psychology teacher telling me that sometimes you have to skip out on the person you're truly in love with because it can be destructive to your life.

Sometimes you have to go for the one who you know you'll be able to build a foundation with. Looking back, what he said makes a lot of sense and I still keep that in mind today.

My mom couldn't stand number two. She and my step father loved the guy I was actually dating at the time but it didn't matter because I loved number two. He actually had me thinking about marrying him. He said he didn't want to have any more kids by anyone else but me. He told me he wanted me to have his son. Today, he has found someone else to handle that task and I'm cool with that. My relationship with the actual guy I was dating at the time started to fade due to the long distance nature of it and there was a possibility that he was moving out of the state. Number two and I continued seeing each other. I eventually met his daughter in person and even spent the night with them.

I continued to keep my options open and every once in a while even went on dates with other guys. We went a full six months without falling out and things were pretty great for the most part. I'd say having a child definitely matured him a bit. It was now three years since we first started talking and our relationship was still a mystery to me. Were we together or not?

My twenty-first birthday was approaching and a different mindset came with that. Could I do better? Yes. Did I have options? Yes. I think he sensed that and it was the main reason we'd stayed cool as long as we did because he knew that I KNEW. However, that didn't stop him from putting his hands on me.

I remember we were walking into his apartment building one night and as we were getting on the elevator the security guard greeted us. I said, "Hi" back and the minute the elevator doors closed he smacked me upside my head and said I was being flirtatious. Now it seems within seconds the elevator doors opened again allowing more people to get on the elevator and so he politely smiled at the others and held my wrist

55

behind my back. So I just knew the minute we entered his apartment, I was going to set it off because I'm not THAT person and refuse to be. We entered his apartment and the minute his apartment door closed, I swung on him and I missed. He caught my wrist and then we started wrestling.

I literally could have seriously hurt him with as much anger that I was feeling inside. It wasn't that the slap hurt because it didn't but I felt disrespected. He, on the other hand thought it was a joke. I continued to see him and he even took me out to dinner for my twenty-first birthday, where I was able to dress up. We partook in a wine tasting, he bought me a cake and everything but the entire time at dinner he kept talking about how he was going to be broke afterwards.

It was such a turnoff but I didn't care because it was my twenty-first birthday and he needed to man up. I just side eyed him and sipped my wine thinking, "I don't care. You're going to pay for this." He was always hopping in my car to go work on his rap career and we drove my car to dinner. I was always doing something for him with no complaints. So, Misha was not trying to hear that.

I had a new air about me at twenty-one years old. I even felt different. I had plans to meet up with some people at the casino after dinner for drinks and of course he let me go alone because he never had any interest to be around any of my friends or family. It's actually come out of his mouth before. Looking back, I should have dropped him sooner for that reason alone.

Name calling is juvenile but these facts are why I always refer to him as "the douchebag" to date, because that's literally what he is. I've never met anyone more terrible than him. He was not willing to compromise at all unless he felt he was going to get something out of it. However, what I've learned is there are so many more people walking this earth that are just like him.

56

Once I turned twenty-one and moved into my own apartment which signaled my new found freedom, I let him go again because I just felt like he was still playing around and I had bigger fish to fry. I had just started a new school to start my program of study and I knew I was passing him up in life. I felt like, "What are you here for? Just to see what you can get out of the situation? He would have me watch his daughter while he went off to do whatever in my car. I was over it.

Once I realized that I'd never be happy with him, I stopped entertaining the thought of a future with him. He even tried to convince me that he was going to start saving up for my ring "next year". At this point I was already aware of the fact that something was seriously off about this guy. I realized that he'd tell me anything.

When he said he was looking for someone to help him take care of the bills, that's when it was

confirmed that he was looking for a woman to take care of him. He had mommy issues and the signs were there from the beginning.

The long talks we use to have into the early morning always were about things that he felt he missed out on in his childhood because of his mom. He was always talking about and blaming his mom for everything but he was super dependent on her as well. I would eventually start going out with a guy that I met at my new school and we were together for three months before I felt like I couldn't deal with him anymore. The relationship got really serious really fast but he had personal issues that included mommy issues along with an alcohol abuse problem that I didn't want to take on. I didn't feel that I deserved to carry those burdens.

Right before breaking up with this guy, I went to have dinner with my first love who happened to know him and so of course he had something to say about the situation. I also met number three right before breaking up with him at the job that I was working at the time. I eventually broke up with the college boyfriend. Number two and I hung out a few more times but I knew that was pretty much dead. We had fun while hanging out but I'd started to redirect my attention to number three who had started to obviously show interest in me.

I saw number two one more time about a month after it was discovered that number three really liked me. It was that last visit that would get number three to admit that he was falling for me and from there things got pretty serious. I haven't seen number two since early 2011. He's reached out to me consistently over the years via social media but I just recently erased him from my Facebook because I could tell by his inbox messages that nothing had changed on his end. He's the past anyway.

Number Three

2011

So...number three is my immediate ex. I met him over five years ago while working my first full-time job during college. It was right at the beginning of that year (2011) and I had received a few new hires to train for the building that I was supervising. He was one of them. Initially, when I'd met him, he told me he was engaged. Over the course of the next month, I'd come to learn so many things about him and because of us having to work closely together, some sort of a bond started to grow.

We began confiding in each other about many things that were going on in our lives…including relationships. I happened to be dating a guy that I'd met at my college at the time but I was pretty much over that relationship and had ended it by the end of the month after meeting number three. Now, my break up with my current boyfriend had nothing to do with number three but it does seem like it happened just in time. We met in January of that year and by February 14th (Valentines Day) in the back of my mind I knew he had something else in mind for us. I'd gotten this notion by the flowers that I received from him. Discreetly of course but they were some of the most beautiful flowers that I'd ever received. I remember it was a random bouquet assembled similarly to wild flowers with a single red rose in the middle of the bouquet.

You see how simple innocent conversations can turn into something more? Now, being the intuitive one, I couldn't help but to think there was a hidden meaning behind this bouquet of flowers and I'm sure there was. From that point forward, I tried to ignore the obvious. I wanted to ignore the chemistry. I did not want to like him, not in a romantic way. He would be the first to express the fact that he was falling for me about a month after the flowers.

I should have known it would be a ride. By the time of this confession, he and his fiancé had broke it off but there was still left over baggage from the situation. I knew but I still went along with it especially after he confessed that he was falling for me. I

Life After 25: Intuitively Me

didn't know which way it would go and was kind of taken back when he initially told me. Me being me, of course I proceeded.

He was cute, and there was this mysterious air about him that I loved. I would eventually come to find out that he's just a deceitful person (like most of the guys I've come across) and apparently likes leading you to believe that things will go in a certain direction. He was good at selling dreams like a used car salesman. I don't think he did that because he was a bad person. I believe he meant well and tried to put something positive out in the atmosphere because there's a part of him that wanted that but old habits die hard.

I felt this way about him because he's probably one of the only guys that I've seriously dated that was not trying to be dependent on me. He never asked or expected anything from me and he always seemed to want to help. At this time in my life, I was so focused on finding a dude with money because I was tired of the bum ass dudes that I was meeting and that's exactly what I got; or so it seemed. Number three, had no issue paying for things and assisting in any way that he could. However, what I came to find out later is that he was somewhat emotionally unavailable.

No matter how much he claimed to love me or helped me financially, he was never really there when he should have been. He was always on the go, shooting a move and doing things with/for everyone else. I always felt like his last priority, because I was. I learned growing up that actions speak louder than words and this particular situation would be what put the nail in the coffin as far as taking people's word as their bond. This would be the situation that would finally wake me up to this particular weakness of mine. I had to learn.

Number three was like a spitting image of my dad in terms of words versus action. Neither of them aren't bad people. In fact they can be some of the coolest people you'll ever meet on a good day. What I mean by that is they're around when things are going the way they want and when they have the opportunity to flaunt but if not, they'll be missing in action. No matter how much they claim to care, in their mind

they're going through something so they can't be bothered. They're both very wishy-washy and two faced. They can tell you one thing and do the complete opposite.

Personally, I can't stand that. One thing about number three is we dated for almost two years straight through and we talked everyday during that time frame.

There are only like two occasions where I remember not hearing from him for a day or so but even then he had someone contact me to keep me in the loop. He made sure to check in with me everyday and throughout each day. I cherished that so much because all I could think about was the fact that my ex never communicated with me by phone this much. We shared stories and lots of laughs daily. It seemed that he was my friend first.

For the first few years, I never suspected him as a deceitful person. It never dawned on me that he probably wasn't being honest with me about anything until his baby mama came into the picture. I was oblivious and in love. I was in love with the future that he was selling me. Like number two, the signs were there from the beginning. I just did not want to see them.

I remember getting pissed time after time again. Pissed about constant broken promises. Like my dad, what kept me going and believing in the fact that he was genuine was the fact that every now and again he would

come through. So, I accepted his excuses for the times that he didn't but I shouldn't have. For example, he kept telling me he wanted to spend the night but always had an excuse as to why he couldn't.

I should have cut ties then. When he showed up to my mom's at 10:45p on Thanksgiving one year, I should have cut ties. When he left me alone on Christmas but kept telling me how he was on his way with my gift, but never showed up. I should have cut ties. He's lived with his mom for majority of our relationship and when he finally did get his own residence, he didn't tell me about it nor would he tell me where he lived. I should have cut ties!

I saw something in him so I couldn't cut ties. Today, I'm not sure what that something is but whatever it was, it kept me holding on. My sister says it was the mystery of him that kept me attracted to the situation. Looking back, that couldn't be any more of a turn off and a red flag but I was younger and did not know any better.

I could go on and on about the things that I went through with this particular individual but I don't want the point to get lost upon you so I'll wrap it up. A lot of the suffering I endured during these relationships could have been avoided had I made alternate decisions and left these characters alone at the first thought of "leaving them alone." I was so concerned with the hurt that I'd feel if they weren't in my life that I didn't consider how much more hurt I'd endure by keeping them there. It was a complete waste of my time and I could have been focused on more important things.

The moral of these stories are exactly as the chapter is titled. "You get what you focus on." I was so in love with the thought of being "in love" and thought that having a boyfriend was "it". When I think about it, that's all I really got from the situation, a boyfriend, not a relationship, not a healthy one anyway. It was only what they wanted me to have.

Obviously, I wasn't worth much to these guys. Probably just something to do, when there was nothing to do. There are so many other things that I could have put my all into. There are so many more things that I could have accomplished and experienced but I missed the opportunities focusing on the wrong things. I want to make it clear that I wasn't giving my all in these relationships either.

I knew better and I never fully trusted myself to do that. However, the saying you are who you attract is a perfect example of why these relationships went the way they did. I was just bullshitting with bullshitters. Had I taken these relationships a bit more seriously, they may have taken me more seriously. There were things that I knew would happen based upon how I assessed the situation.

I knew better but many times I was just too lazy to do better and stand by my standards. You have to put your foot down ladies. If you know you're treading in shady territory, just turn around and avoid it all together. Don't let loneliness or boredom get you in a situation you can't bounce back from. I've been blessed enough to bounce back from every disappointment and heartache but a lot of people aren't able to say the same. Protect your heart and your boundaries. I promise you have nothing to lose as long as you keep your morals and self-respect in check.

What I want you to take away from this chapter:

- Examine the three scenarios that I've given you and compare the similarities and differences

- Are there things in your life in which you've given entirely too much attention to?

- Think about what's really of priority to you and focus on that and that alone. Everything else will come in its right time

Chapter 5

I Will Not Apologize For Evolving Past Your Comfort Zone

Early 2016

To piggy back off of the last chapter "You get what you focus on so focus on what you want", my primary focus has always been success. Therefore school was always a high priority. It's the reason I am where I am today. I'm twenty-six. I have I have my bachelor's degree. Everything I have is in my name and I have stable employment. Everyone will not be rooting for your success. There will be people that are intimidated by your drive.They will try to dull your sparkle. By making you feel like you're doing too much or will try to redirect the attention off of your accomplishments by making you feel bad about it.

You may bring a recent accomplishment to someone's attention and in that moment, they'll decide to bring up something negative to redirect the attention from you. Pay attention to people like that. From high school graduation on through my college years, I started to see it more and more. I was constantly accused of thinking I was " better". Why was I being cast out for accomplishing things that I should have been accomplishing at my age? But see, that's the thing.

People will try to make you appear to be the weird one, bougie, or the lame one for living righteously. There is nothing wrong with being the good boy/girl because later on everyone will be wishing they were you. You have to remember to stay focused. What's crazy is you'll motivate a lot of people with your drive and achievements but there will be people who should be in your corner that low-key won't. It just comes with success and growing.

The number one key to success is AMBITION. Everyone doesn't have it but it is a behavior that can be learned and can definitely be taught. I pride myself on pushing people to be more ambitious, hence my brand Ambitious Mix. Who doesn't want to be successful in everything that they do? No one's going to admit to that but there are people whose actions scream "I don't want to be successful." Not that it's done intentionally but these are the vibes the they give off—stay away from these type of people. They're usually progress killers.

You'll have people that expect you to be more supportive of them than they are of you and will even try to pick fights with you about it. I'm really big on "treating people how you want to be treated." It's a value that I was raised with and that I still continue to live on. I'm not going to be anymore supportive to you then you are to me. Unfortunately, there are many ornery and self-centered people walking this earth and they'll never see things from the perspective that I'm presenting to you here today.

These type of people will always view themselves as the exception. Meaning, they'll always view themselves as the exception and think regardless of the shitty behavior they exhibit towards people, they should be accepted"as is" without consequence. While I'm all for accepting people as they are, I do not believe in being

around someone that isn't good for my spirit or my mental. These are the consequences that sometimes come with people accepting people as they are. Other people dislike being around them.

No one really likes being around a self-serving person, regardless of what you see and hear. Keep an eye out for people that make you feel like you owe them an explanation for every little thing that you do. You have to learn to stop letting your left hand know what your right hand is doing. Some people solely exist in your life to

dull your sparkle. Those people want to know what you're thinking about doing before you do it so they can sabotage and/or stop you. Their efforts won't be obvious because they're usually posing as a friend, family member, and sometimes a loved one (unfortunately).

I saw a meme on Facebook by Steven Aitchison that read: "You don't owe anyone an explanation for your level of education, where you live, your appearance, your political views, your belief in GOD, your alone time, and your life and/or relationship choices." I really love this message because it is true to life. You can't let people's expectations of you define you.

I believe that sometimes God puts you in people's life as a blessing but not the blessing that people think. I believe God will put you in several people's lives to make them uncomfortable. You'll be a blessing to many people's lives and they won't even realize it. They'll instead be mad, feel some type of way and/or be envious of you. You'll be as nice of a person as you can be to them and they'll still envy you.

They'll envy you because you'll be a constant reminder of everything they're not. They'll despise you because you did things the correct way and it worked. They'll make you out to be their enemy because you possess something they want but they'll never understand how you're a blessing to their life. They'll struggle to understand why you make them so uncomfortable and may completely ignore the feeling altogether.

It's not for you to take personal because it's an issue that's bigger than you. You can be as supportive and encouraging as you want with these type of people but they'll still try to cover up the fact that it's them and not you. You're crazy if you actually believe that. The goal is to become so confident in who you are as a person that it does not matter what anyone has to say about you. Never let anyone dull your sparkle!

What I want you to take away from this chapter:

- Be true to yourself and never let anyone dull your sparkle.

- People will have their opinions regardless.

- Don't take everything personally. Sometimes, it's really not you.

Chapter 6

I'm Nothing Like This Generation, I Just Live In It

Do you ever feel like an outsider in your own environment? Are you the black sheep of your circle? Why is that? Is it because you avoid crowds and prefer authenticity? Perhaps, you're not a follower and that's what people dislike about you the most.

How dare you have your own mind with morals in tact?

I'll be the first to admit that life is no walk in the park. The hardest part is simply dealing with people as a whole. You're not always going to be surrounded with people that you see eye to eye with. In fact, no one will ever truly get you unless you're pretty basic as a person. If you're lucky, there may be one person that truly gets you and often times people label this person as their "soulmate".

Not everyone gets one and some are even considered lucky if they find one. Well I don't know about you, but I've always sort of felt out of place. For years, I've joked about being born a decade later then I should have been. I've accepted the fact that perhaps I'm an old soul. After all, I've been told several times while growing up that I'm mature for my age.

I've accepted that. I'm pretty responsible and I always try to do the right thing. I'm definitely what you would label a modern "good girl". I don't have a police record and I've never been handed a ticket. I went to college and graduated with my bachelor's degree.

I don't have kids yet and don't plan to until I'm married. On paper, I am the example. I'm am the poster child for how it should be, yet I'm sticking out like a sore thumb. Yes, there are other people that have accomplished some of the same things that I have but there are far more who have not and society has made those people an acceptation. It is considered cool to do things the fast way instead of the right way.

Society has instilled an "act now, think later mentality" in this new generation so they don't want to work or do much of anything for that matter. They just want rewards

and will get it by any means necessary. Yet, they can give another advice on how they should bc living their life and not be doing anything that makes them credible on

giving advice. This new generation has the gift of gab. All talk and no action. I'm aware of the inauthenticity and these are just a few things that I have to ignore on the day to day basis because when you're genuine but dealing with deceitful people you can either try to beat them by staying true to yourself or join them. Sometimes I find myself feeling like I have to be fake with fake people, and act oblivious to the obvious, just to avoid confrontation.

Other times, I just prefer to not be bothered with society at all. It seems the older I get the more introverted I become. Sometimes, I feel like there is too much going on and the overstimulation of my brain from having to process so much inauthentic info on the daily is exhausting. If you've found yourself feeling this way then I'd suggest getting comfortable with being alone. Learn to love your alone time.

It is the best way to refresh your batteries and to learn to deal with things as most people tend to think a lot when they're alone.Use that time to reflect. Use that time to work on yourself. No one likes to be around needy people all the time because it's draining. Don't be the person who sucks the energy out of people and situations. You'll just end up alone anyhow, that is if you refuse to change your ways. There's nothing wrong with being independent. If you can't do something yourself, then you

don't deserve anything. I do not think people should receive handouts whatsoever. Anything that you desire, you should be able to achieve yourself.

Even when it comes down to the smallest thing such as asking for help. Instead of expecting a free handout, be prepared to compensate that person…even if you just treat them to a nice dinner. My mom always told me, "Nothing in life is free." She told me that so that I'd learn the value of hard work, and that I did.

While writing this chapter, I'm sitting on my patio which resides in one of the wealthiest (if not the wealthiest) cities in Wayne County, MI. A city that is predominantly white and from what I'm told use to be a very prejudice town, yet across the street from where I'm sitting, I see a group of children playing (both African American and White) and they're having such a good time with each other just doing old fashioned kids' stuff. That made my heart smile. Let's get back to the

simple times before the millennium and all the technology craze. Let's simply get back to enjoying life without all the complications.

I crave simplicity because I'm a simple person. Now, that's not to be confused with basic. There's a difference between being simple and basic but that's another topic for another day. To be honest, that's what attracted me to move to the city I live in now. It was not my first option but I took a leap out on faith and have grown to love it here.

I remember having a conversation about this very town long before I decided to move here a few years ago. I was considering it and a few other towns because my first choice did not have any apartments available. I was at my company's holiday mixer and was having a conversation with a guy who worked for the company my company did business with and he just so happened to live in the city that I currently live in. When I told him that I was considering moving to this particular city, he suggested I live somewhere with a more active night life due to me being a single young female. He thought I'd be bored living in a family-oriented town.

To be honest, that's what solidified my decision to move here. As I explained to that guy, I'd rather commute to the fun and then come back home where it's safe and quiet rather than to live in the heat of everything. In my opinion, there's a time and place for everything. Partying is not and has never been my number one priority. It may have seemed weird to him but as this chapter is titled, "I'm nothing like this generation, I just live in it."

People have to realize that there are still some people in this generation who live by traditional values. Not everyone is living unconventional. Some of us just dare to be different and want to stand alone. Our identity is everything as well as a respectable reputation. Some of us don't concern ourselves with the bullshit. We focus on what's important and act accordingly. Be yourself. Be great and never lose yourself. Stay true to your beliefs and don't feel pressured to fit in because sometimes being the black sheep is the best thing that can happen to you.

What I want you to take away from this chapter:

- Don't feel out of place if you're not interested in doing things that your peers are doing

- Stand in your truth

- Be proud of what sets you apart from the next person.

- Despite what other's think, remember, it's all about what you want for yourself so don't give up on that.

Chapter 7

Walking By Faith Is The Best Workout

"Walk by faith and not by sight." -2 Corinthians 5:7, The Holy Bible.

One of the best pieces of advice that you could ever receive in life can be found in the bible (Basic Instructions Before Leaving Earth). This is the perfect acronym for the exact thing this famous universal book does. You can find a story that pertains to just about everything you have or will go through during your life. I had never experienced what it truly meant to walk by faith until the summer of 2015. I'm a planner so I've always had faith that I'd accomplish certain things and I made certain decisions that put me on the right path to achieving those things.

It wasn't until last year, when I grew depressed working at a job where I knew there was no opportunity for growth, that I truly understood what it meant to walk by faith. I kept trying to stick it out. Friends and family told me to stick it out and to make sure I had another job lined up before I quit. No one understood that I was literally depressed going into work altogether. I was always on the brink of tears and just tired all together. What really did it for me was the thirty-six cent raise that I was given with no opportunity to object because my manager had me under the impression that I was not getting one.

By the time I was informed of the measly raise, I had already signed the paper work. So, I could not object because I had already signed the papers. I'm sure even you could see what happened there. I was mentally done after that situation. I knew I was going to quit and so I needed to find another job soon. Our department was short staffed so we were being over worked (particular me because everyone else in the department was older and slow). It was a stressful environment. One day, I did something that I thought I'd never do. I quit my job on spot without a two week notice.

Aside from other people quitting, something happened a few days before that leading me to my decision. A situation occurred in which my manager did not go to bat for me like she should have and I was already feeling drained.I wanted to quit that day but I went home and then called in the next day. I figured maybe I just needed a break away from there and when I got back I'd be over it. Well, the morning I got back, something else happened that ruffled my feathers and once again, my manager did not go to bat for me even when I wasn't in the wrong. By 9:30am I had quit my job.

I was pulled into an office with my manager who I felt came at me all wrong. Without even knowing the whole story she immediately took the other persons side and tried to send me home for a few days.I told her I'm not coming back. She asked for a resignation letter and I told her I had one typed up in the car ready to go. I actually did, I'd typed up a resignation letter when the first incident happened a few days earlier. She looked surprised as I knew she would. I gathered all of my things at my desk and I left.

I never brought her the resignation letter by the way. I walked out that building and never looked back. I had no job lined up, no extra savings, just the money in my account and I wasn't sure what my next move would

be but I wasn't worried. I couldn't be worried because in my heart I knew GOD had me. I really believed that everything would work out in my favor.

In the back of my mind, I thought, "Worse case scenario: If I don't find job in a month, then I'll just pack up my cat and belongings and we're going to leave Michigan." I knew if I could not find a job to pay my bills, I'd have to forfeit my lease but that'd be something I'd just have to deal with later. Either way, I had an optimistic outlook. Whatever happened, I knew I'd adapt either way. I did not allow myself to worry and I didn't tell anyone because I did not want them judging or

worrying me. I ended up being unemployed for an entire month which was my deadline and it turned out to be one of the best months of my life.

Let me tell you about it, I published a book, and I simply was able to sit back and enjoy the simple things in life worry-free.

I had courage to do these things because God spoke to me that March. He told me I could have whatever I wanted in a year and a half but I couldn't stay where I was. During that time in my life, there were so many things that I wanted to let go of and

start fresh so it was that confirmation that helped me move forward. It helped me let go of things that were now stale and irrelevant to my future successes.

The actual letting go was the hardest part. I started my journey by letting go of a person. A person that I needed to let go of permanently a long time ago but even after I thought I let them go the first time, they somehow inserted themselves back into my life. Well, I won't say it like I don't know how it happened. We're all adults so we can at least be honest with ourselves.

We do things and allow things because we want the familiar rather than the new because it scares us. We know what we're getting with the familiar and we get comfortable with that. We think we know how to deal with it and therefore allow poisonous people and situations to keep reentering our lives or we never really leave at all. We're scared of new beginnings because we look at getting rid of deadweight as a loss. We think we're losing something if we give it up but what we have to realize is we can't hold on to every single thing that we're handed in life.

How will we have room for improvements? If I'm holding on to something but I desire more or better, why would I still hold on to something that no longer serves me a purpose or any happiness for that matter? Many of us have an issue letting things go because we're territorial and attached to it. We feel like "It's mine," and we don't want to let anyone else have it. Whether it's a relationship, friendship, job or tangible item, what's ours is ours.

It's the reason some people live as hoarders. Everything that comes into their possession, they want to hold onto it forever. Many of us do this with relationships, jobs, friendships etc. Think of your peace of mind and goals, and put them in the forefront of everything that you do. What makes you truly happy?

Whatever it is, that is what you need to be after at all times. You should always be chasing your happiness and peace of mind. If ever you're in a situation that brings you both happiness and a peace of mind (consistently) then you've struck gold! If that's not the case then it's time to let go and move on. It really is as simple as that.

It goes back to that whole self-love and knowing your worth ideology. You're happiness and peace of mind should always be top priority. I defeat my struggles when I remind myself of that.

As an adult, I understand that Depression is an actual diagnosis and condition. There are certain behaviors that can help one distinguish if this is something that they're experiencing. I was going into a job everyday that I grew to hate because we were being overworked and my department was short staffed. Aside from the fact that people were quitting or getting fired left and right, it made it that more stressful. There was no opportunity for growth within the company which you're mislead about during the hiring process.

I worked there for two years and only called off once due to a snowstorm. Initially, I was excited to work for the company. The perks were great. The PTO structure was generous. However, I was not working in my purpose and what happened going forward changed my life. I started dreading going into work. I was already stressed from the pressure of getting caught up and on deadline as we were super understaffed. I would wake up in the morning and just lay there because I didn't want to get out of bed. I wouldn't get up until the very last minute and would get to work just in enough time to not be considered late but some days I would be late and I

didn't care. Some days I'd be crying getting out of bed and I'd just sit there and talk to God.

Each day became harder and harder. It changed my mood outside of work. I didn't want to be bothered or talk to anyone and I started sleeping a lot. However, it wasn't just my job, I was also dealing with a dead end relationship. I was convinced by the other person to give it another shot when once again it turned out to be a complete waste of time.

I struggled with my initial feelings for this person because they were there for me at a time in my life when I really needed someone but overtime I outgrew that person because they still was not the right person for me. I spent over a year's time apart from this person after our first break-up (which took place after I graduated from college). Eventually, we found our way back to each other but it was more so a lesson than a blessing. Perhaps, it was a form of closure. I'm not sure but what I do know is everything happens for a reason.

During our period of trying to work it out, I was also going through disliking my job. He kept telling me to stick it out and kill them with kindness and so on. I was telling him that I wanted to start my own business but he didn't hear me. I even tried to include him in on it. I asked for his support in simply spreading the word and as polite and indirect as he could put it, he said no.

Now again, we've spent some time apart, so we've grown and learned different sides about each other. I've learned that people behave differently with different people. This person that claimed to love me and care about my well being who I always gave credit for being there during a time in my life when I needed someone, was not as supportive as I initially thought. I had to finally accept that he wasn't as supportive of me as he was with other people. This is something that I always knew in the back of my mind so why did this particular event need to happen for me to finally accept that he's not someone I need in my life? I also started to see that he's never going to change. When it comes to me, he's going to deal with me however he

feels and it's up to me to take it or leave it. He did the typical, The first month or two he had convinced me that things would be different.

He even showed me things that he had not shown me before but eventually I saw that old habits die hard. I am proud to say that HE was the first leap of faith I took. I decided to move on for good. I said what I needed

to say via text because eventually he started to become unreachable for whatever reason and I haven't looked back since. We've ran into each other in traffic and he just recently reached out to me on Facebook early 2016, to "make sure I was ok," like why wouldn't I be? You're no longer a dark cloud over my life.

Of course, he tried to find a way to discourage me once again by telling me he thinks I'm too smart to be working for the company I'm working for and how I should have just went back to school. I was literally tickled by that comment and said, "I'll show him." When people try to throw salt on what you're doing, use that salt as

ammunition and let the haters drive you to your successes. Once I cut that string loose in 2015, I started focusing on my career again and in what direction I wanted to take it.

I had more time to myself to focus on what I needed to be focused on at the moment. More doors started to open for me. I launched my business, Ambitious Mix LLC, a media services company, and offered services related to what I have my degree in as I'm credible and seasoned in those areas. It made the most sense. The Ambitious Mix brand already existed through my blog but I had received some wonderful advice from a business associate (as I am a client of theirs).

She suggested I incorporate especially if I was spending money to run my blog. Of course it made sense. I need to be getting a return on my investment and so I did.

I started building a business around my blog's brand. I had no idea what was to follow after but I was focused and I had faith which would eventually lead me up to the day I quit my job (which was the second thing I let go). "You can have whatever you want in a year in a half but you can't stay where you are," God told me. He wanted to me clean up my social life and business life so that I could move forward and make room for what was due to come into my life. I also noticed He started rearranging who I spent my time with. He distanced certain friends and brought new friends into my life whose goals closely aligned with mine.

I saw it happening before my eyes and all I wanted to do was obey His orders. I knew something better was coming and so I was going to do whatever I could to get that better and God was helping me through my obedience. I attended church service as always and just remained positive but it was only a matter of time before I became bothered again and it was because I was walking into a job everyday that served me no purpose. I was listening to business podcasts and as the days went on I thought about quitting more.

I didn't have a job lined up though and everyone kept telling me "no matter what you do, don't quit your job if you don't have another job lined up." They didn't understand. They didn't understand because they weren't going through it. It's easy to offer advice when you're not personally going through it. People will give you advice based on their own fears and lack of faith.

In my mind, I kept reminding myself that I always find a job yet I could not line something up to get out of here. I was convinced that it was because I was always at work and if I just had some time to take off, I'd for sure land something. The more I thought about that, the more fearless I became. I knew there was a possibility that I'd have to quit this job without having another one lined up because I told myself no matter what, I'd be gone before fall. I wanted to be gone within the next thirty days but I had to do it at the right time. The urge grew in me more each day but I was convinced that I'd be ok. I believed that.

I believed the prophecy that God sent me. He'd never let me down. I just had to truly have faith. I had to erase fear and just do what I had to do. I look back on that time in my life as one of great transformation.

I did something I had never done in my life and it turned out in my favor like I believed it would. I had no money saved up just what was in my account from the previous pay check and a few hundred dollars from a wedding I had just worked. I lived off that for a whole month. I did get behind in some bills but I was able to withdraw my 401k that I took up with that company so by the time I was receiving my first paycheck from my new job I also had that money to help me catch up in addition to my paycheck. It was tight for me for about a month after I started my new job but I managed and it's been smooth sailing since then. Would you look at GOD!

You see, God didn't place that prophesy on me for nothing. He wanted me to understand that it was time to let go of what was comfortable for me and to trust that better things are coming. Let's not forget, I self-published my first book through amazon.com and that happened the month that I was unemployed. Interesting the things you can accomplish when you free yourself from distractions and put your faith in GOD. I can't wait to see what he does for me in the years to come.

What I want you to take away from this chapter:

• Do not be afraid of the unknown. I was like this for years and I believe it slowed my progress.

• Take chances and have faith that everything will work out as it should.

• Be fearless. If something does not feel right, get away from it. Do what's best for you!

Chapter 8

Change Your Perspective: Positive Vibes Only

What's the meaning of life? Personally, I feel that I've discovered this frequently asked question a couple of years ago while tapping into my mental. The brain is a muscle. Am I correct? There is no limit as to how much we can build on this muscle because you can never know too much. Unlike, regular muscles it is not deemed unhealthy to be constantly building upon the brain.

Think about those gross body-builders that get too big and start having fitness related injuries. Luckily, this is not the case with your brain. However, the smarter you become, the weirder you appear to people because you typically start to do things that are not of the norm.

Upon thinking about these things I also began to think about perception versus reality, how things are, what we make of them, and how we perceive them. Do you ever think about the rich versus the poor and the difference between how each lives their life? For many there is no difference. How is it that someone who'd be deemed poor by society appears to be just as happy if not happier than someone whose stinking rich and should not have a care in the world? The Answer: Perception is reality for most.

The meaning of life and the lives we live is all in our perspective. It's all in our minds. Everything is in our mind. It's how we're able to see something that someone else doesn't see and so on. Life is perspective. What's important to you?

Ask yourself that and then think about things that have happened to you in your life. Would you have been affected the same if those things that are important to you were no longer important? This world, this entire universe is in our mind. All of this is a creation of ours. We created all of this with our minds. What we see is what we want to see. My world probably looks a lot different from your world. We may see the same things but no doubt, we view them differently.

I see this all the time when I witness an argument or a disagreement happening. Two people were present for the same event yet can't seem to see eye to eye on what

actually happened. How are we even functioning out in society when there are people that see things differently than ourselves? Somehow we do.

The remedy is to have an open mind and to change your perspective as needed. Remind yourself, that it's positive vibes only. You must remain positive at all times even when something unfortunate happens. Be optimistic as often as you can. That is how the poor man is able to live a life as happy as the filthy rich millionaire.

People say, "more money, more problems," and I agree to a certain extent. However, one must consider what's important to them? What's a problem, and what's not a real issue? I feel as though people create their own problems mentally and it almost always has to do with greed and being unfocused on the bigger picture. To those who are considered wealthy due to simply having more funds in their account than the average person, what is it that troubles you so much in a world where money is not an issue?

Is it the fake family members and friends that all of a sudden have taken an extreme interest in you due to your boasting about the things that you have? Does it surprise you that they're always asking for favors no matter how outrageous they may be? Guess what, if you were a poorer version of you, people would still ask you for things

and what would your reaction be? The favors may be less extreme but would the poorer version of you be more prone to say, "Yes" or would it depend on what they're asking for?

A poor man can still be a target for robbery as well as a rich man can. A poor man can be surrounded by as many users as a rich man can. If people think they can get it from you, they're going to ask and there's nothing you can do about it. What you can do something about is your attitude, how well you adapt to situations, and your reaction. These things aren't really problems unless we accept them as so.

Now, I'm not suggesting you be in denial about everything. What I'm simply pointing out is YOUR life is what you make of it. If you're feeling down about things

that have recently happened to you or the way your life is going, change your perspective and choose happiness—that's right, you can choose to be happy!

Our lives are based upon the Laws of Attraction. If you can see the worse in every situation then you're typically what people consider a pessimist. If you think negatively, the negative will continue to happen to you. You can't be negative about everything and expect positive things to happen for you. You are what you attract and that goes for friends, romantic relationships, and career progression.

If you've been the type of person that always puts out negative vibes then that's what you're going to keep getting back. If you're that person, I need you to stop being like that! If you know someone like this, tell them to stop being like that! People make excuses and say they can't change when really they won't change. Anyone can change.

Behaviors are based on habit. People behave the way they're use to behaving because it's easier. Instead of choosing to do things differently, they choose to do what they're use to doing in fear of stepping out of their comfort zone. Habits CAN be changed through repetition. The more you do something—the more you'll do something.

What I want you to take away from this chapter:

•   Paradigm shifts are necessary to progress in life

•   Habits can be changed

•   Everything is in your mind so control your thoughts and adapt to situations accordingly

Chapter 9

Communication Kills Assumption

Do you ever think, "Wow, it seems like everyone is happy, carefree, and doing better than me?"

Most of that isn't true, especially the carefree part. If you see someone doing what you want to be doing, reach out to them. You'd be surprised at what you find out. Most people post the good stuff. Rarely, will you ever see the struggle documented (or we just don't pay attention to it).

We assume these people have these things because they were dealt better cards in life. Instead of assuming, ask some of these people how they got to where they are today and I bet your perspective changes. It may even motivate you more! Often times we assume instead of actually finding out the facts. I recently had a conversation with a loved one about assuming before communicating. They'd brought something to my attention about another loved one that they had no factual proof on and was just going off of assumption.

I actually knew for a fact that they were misreading things due to just recently talking to the party involved. After revealing the info I knew, my loved one seemed to have been surprised by the info that I shared. Of course my suggestion was that a conversation needed to be had.

"You cannot assume something about someone for the simple fact, you have no idea what they're going through or what demons they're battling."

My very words were just that. So, why do people assume? In my opinion, assumption comes from laziness and being ornery. People want to believe everything is about them and so assumption is easier for them because they don't want to do any leg work. It's easier to make something up and run with it than to address the inquiry and find out for sure.

It's always been funny to me that people are so comfortable taking something and running with it rather than finding out for sure. It's messy and judgmental. What I've come to realize about civilization is most are super judgmental even though it clearly

states in the bible to not judge anyone —That's GOD's job — yet most of us do it everyday without even realizing. I'm really big on communication so I really want to dig deep on this topic.

I want you guys to get out of assuming things. You'll block your blessings doing that. What I'm talking about specifically is having a lack of faith in what you do. Assuming things are going to go a certain way because you've never done it or it happened that way before. Stop assuming, especially when it comes to your business endeavors.

Believe it or not, I want you to succeed at all that your heart desires! You're probably thinking, "Ok, now she doesn't know me from a can of paint." I don't have to know you personally to wish you the best. It's just the way I was raised and it's part of the reason I started the Ambitious Mix blog. I wanted to inspire others while sharing stories and general information that would hopefully help my readers take the necessary steps to make their dreams come true.

It literally gives me life to hear and see other people doing well. So, I want you all to have real faith in what you do. Just because you don't have the confidence, don't assume that things aren't going to work out for you the way you intend. Be positive and simply have faith. When you assume in business, it lowers your enthusiasm and you don't work as hard at it because you assume that you already know that outcome.

There is a difference between assuming everything will work out and actually working towards it. Faith without works is dead. Never forget that. If something doesn't work out the way you want it to, it's because you didn't want it to work out. Especially if you just sat around assuming.

What I want you to take away from this chapter:

- If you want something bad enough, find out who you need to get in contact with. Communicate with them to best find out how to go about it and then do it!

- **How to best communicate:** Present what it is that you're trying to find out to the appropriate source and then just sit there and LISTEN. I mean really listen to what they're telling you and analyze every bit of it so that you can process it effectively and apply it accordingly. The best way to communicate is to listen. It's the only way to understand.

Chapter 10

Less Relationship Goals: More Self Goals

Isn't it obvious? Being in a relationship with someone is and has been the most important thing to accomplish to the average person. Whether they're ready to be in a relationship or not, people just want someone or something to claim. No matter what they have to go through to get it let alone keep it, we're programed to want and need a romantic relationship. As if that's really going to complete us. Some believe that it does but I beg to differ.

Relationships are flaky and aren't a guarantee. Society has been trying to find the formula for years. What makes a relationship last? How can I stay married to someone forever without getting tired of them? Is monogamy real?

These are legit questions and people in today's world want to know. Times are very different now. People don't really value the sanctity of marriage and are often times only a willing participant for the wedding ceremony and the benefits that come along with it after the fact, security. It's something we all look for because it makes us live comfortably knowing that we're secure.

We must start doing better as a society though. For one, GOD is watching. What we're experiencing here on this earth is not permanent and can be taken away at any given moment. You can't be "rich and piss-poor morally."

My primary goal has always been to stay in touch with myself. If I'm not sure of who I am, how can I try to convince others to address me in a a certain fashion? I can't. You can't sell something you're not confident in so why not focus on being confident in yourself first and foremost?

For instance, I'm in a relationship but that doesn't mean it's time to stop doing what I've already set out to do. I'm not going to forfeit my personal goals because of a relationship. I still have to grow and develop as a person for me to be useful to anyone else. Anyone that doesn't get that is probably already failing at life. You should always be working on yourself, point blank period.

How can this be accomplished? Spend time alone. You can't work on yourself if you're always with someone 24/7. For instance, I had some time to myself this past Sunday. I took a nice, much needed, nap to give my brain some rest.

Once I got up, I decided to roll out my Yoga mat to meditate. I closed my eyes and took a deep breath a few times before pulling out my bible and prayer journal. I spread those across the yoga mat as well. I grabbed a bottle of water and put my ItWorks greens in my water so that I could alkalize, detox and balance while meditating on God's word.

It was one of the most wonderful experiences that I'd ever experienced in life. As simple as that was, it relaxed me and truly gave me the opportunity to value my alone time. It was a great time for reflection,

which is a must and it calmed me. I recommend meditating at least once a week. However you decide to meditate, whether it be yoga or listening to audio, DO IT and thank me later.

I actually had a great conversation with a customer earlier as I had to take him to a specific location to complete our business. In the car ride over, we talked about how he could feel my vibrations and he knew what type of person I was because of it. He said he figured my birthday was in August because of the way I interacted with people. We talked about self-awareness and being one with ourselves. We talked

about how many lack self-awareness and do not realize that this is the key to growth and to reaching success at any heights. It was a pretty enlightening conversation and I just thank God for those random people I meet out in the world who truly get it. I tend to instantly click with these type of people. Then of course, I never see them

again but it's nice to know that there are others that have the same perspective and spiritual beliefs as myself. It's interesting how we can almost instantly recognize each other simply off of vibes alone.

He also brought up the fact that he knew I was a number one. Now, I had no idea what he was referring to so I asked. It turns out he was referring to numerology. Now, I'm familiar with astrology but I've never gotten so deep that I've studied numerology. I don't even dabble in astrology anymore due to my stronger relationship with GOD.

Of course, I looked up what he was referring to out of curiosity once I got home. Would you believe it? His theory about me in regard to being a one was dead on. It describes my personality almost to a tee. It's crazy how some people are so in tune with the universe that they can read you that easily. These aren't things that I study or even dabble in at this point in my life but it's almost scary how these "ologies" can describe the characteristics of a person based off of when they were born. It was a positive experience to say the least and whether I completely agreed with his belief system, which he also happened to be GOD fearing and attended church regularly, I still listened to him intently because the goal is to seek to understand. The interesting part was he never went into grave detail about it, he just gave me a number.

There definitely was a reason for that meeting. I mean, everything happens for a reason right? I think it happened to help me reflect more on who I am as a person and how it's perceived by others. The reason I think so is because I later read a book at lunch that pointed out that very thing as well. No lie.

I always know when GOD is trying to tell me something because often times I'll keep seeing the same message presented to me multiple times. It's like He knows I can be a bit stubborn so I have to see it a few times for it to click. I appreciate and am so grateful for God's patience with me. It has developed me into such a remarkable woman. Keep working on yourself. It's so worth it!

What I want you to take away from this chapter:

• Your peace of mind should always be top priority

• You cannot find peace or happiness in someone else

• Self-Love is the best love first and foremost

• God is always working on you so he needs you to partner with him and work on you too!

Chapter 11

Be Consistent, Hard Work Pays Off

I couldn't wait to get to this chapter. I can confidently speak on this topic because I know first hand that consistency got me to where I am today. Inconsistency makes me uncomfortable. It's a sure sign of disorganization which makes me cringe. The only way to truly be organized is to be consistent.

Ever since I was a little girl, I knew almost the exact direction my life would take. I knew I would graduate high school and go on to college. I knew I would end up being this sophisticated business woman. Traveling and writing about my experiences would be priority and I'd simply be happy just living the life I want to live. My life isn't too far off from what I saw as a child.

I've pretty much done all that I knew I would accomplish. I just took another route to get there. The road got a little bumpy at times but GOD made sure I made it to my desired destination every time. He's making sure of the "now" as I take this journey to the next level. I've learned through consistency that I can be whatever I want and do whatever I want as long as I put my mind to it.

For instance, I graduated college in 4 years and 4 months(just an extra semester but pretty much on time) and that was only due to changing my minor last minute. Other than that, I pretty much graduated on time.

I did my four years and I was out of there. Are you wondering how I did it?

You should be asking yourselves how I did it with so much going on. I was in school full-time, working part-time and then full-time, and managing a house hold at one point (cat included).

What kept me going was consistency. Consistency eventually created habit and out of habit I continued to wake up and go to school everyday despite personal things that were going on. Embracing consistency gives you the opportunity to get things done as you'll begin to do them out of habit and on auto-pilot (without even thinking about it). Next thing you know, you'll look around and you'll be exactly where you want to be. Now this is also true when consistently doing things that are not conducive to your success.

If you consistently do non-productive things, it becomes habit and you'll do these things on a regular basis without even realizing how much it's setting you back because it's become your norm. For instance, those that are habitual liars tend to think the "lies" aren't lies. They don't see why your reaction is what it is because they do it out of habit without even realizing that they're doing it. They get offended when confronted about it and have a hard time understanding why you're coming at them the way that you are.

School has always been important to me. Even when I didn't want to go to school, most times I got up and went. It was like a job to me. It was just something that I had to do. My mom would always say, "I know I don't have to worry about you getting up for school. Now, your brother on the other hand…"

It was second nature to me. Growing up, school was a requirement. It was a normal part of life's process. I'd really have to be sick sick to miss a day and I'm the same way now with my job. Even when I was legit sick,

I'd try to go to school just to end up getting sent home. I wasn't a quitter and I tried hard to stay in routine in order to keep things ordinary for myself.

To be consistent got harder once I got older. I just wrote a blog post speaking on this very idea that it was just easier as a child because you always had something to look forward to. You looked forward to growing up and learning new things. You looked

forward to seeing your friends and didn't have a care in the world for the most part. Things are opposite for us now as adults.

Remember when we were kids and we looked forward to another school year. We were excited to be in the classroom with our friends, to see where our assigned seats would be…if we had assigned seats. The classroom would be filled with colorful pictures that teach us things and we'd soak it in while awaiting lunch in eagerness hoping it was Taco Tuesday. The most important event over anything else was planning our first day of school outfit because first impressions last.

We use to be excited just waking up in the morning because the tomorrow that we were looking forward to had just become TODAY We got another chance to live, be around people that we love and there was always something to look forward to. How do we get away from this as we age? We become adults, we dread waking up in the

morning to go to work and we procrastinate when it comes to simply getting things done.

We procrastinate because we don't want to do it. What happened to our enthusiasm? Why are we not doing things we actually want to do? We should be eager to wake up each day knowing we're going to see people we love. We should still look forward to learning new things everyday, after all, that's the only way we'll grow right? Expanding our understanding and perspective further develops us as humans but we can't do that if we're always looking at the glass as half empty.

As children we were more hopeful because we knew anything was possible. We knew we could be whatever we wanted when we grew up and we often used our imagination to see things that weren't quite there. We envisioned our desires this way and it motivated us each and everyday thus affecting our behavior and reactions towards everyday life happenings. What's motivating us these days? Are we motivated by things that directly affect our desires?

Or are we just skating by everyday? Are you alive or are you truly living? If you've lost your enthusiasm over the years, don't worry! You can get it back but it's going to

require you to reset your system. It's going to require you to revisit your original way of doing things.

Tap into your inner child and get back to the bright side!
The bright side is what's going to help you become consistent. If you become an optimist, you will always have something to look forward to. Even when bad things happen, you won't let that deter you from your goals because an optimist is going to remember to focus on the bigger picture. Consistency is key. Habits fuel consistency and your attitude drives your habits.

Ask yourself, "What's important to me?" Take a look at what you've been consistently doing all these years. Is that all that's really important to you or have you been focused on the wrong things? If in fact you've been consistently working towards what's important to you, do an audit anyway. Are you putting as much time into what you're passionate about as you can?

Evaluate the areas of your life. Where are you able to subtract time from to make more time for what's most important to you? Find out sooner rather than later and

address that. Consistency makes things come to life. Just be careful what you're giving consistency to.

What I want you to take away from this chapter:

- Consistency is one of the major keys of success.
- Create positive and productive habits and be consistent with your goals.
- You can accomplish what ever you want as long as you work at it every day. Inconsistency slows down progress.

Chapter 12

Create The Life You Want

You can do what ever you put your mind to. This is something I was told since I was a little girl. I've carried that with me throughout my life. It's what motivates me and keeps me going. I know that with hard work and discipline, I can have all that my heart desires.

It's all about strategy and implementation. You have to make precise moves to get what you want. Meaning, everything that you do should directly align with the life that you're trying to create for yourself. In addition to what was discussed in the previous chapter, this all goes hand in hand with creating the life you want. How can I create the life I want?

I discuss 12 Ambitions in my first book *Ambition For Sale*. The principles discussed in that book will help you create the life you want. It'll help you locate your golden egg. It'll change your perspective on any thing and you'll put it down feeling more productive as you will have started creating productive habits by the end of the book. My goal here is to make you more Ambitious because ambition is what's going to drive you to create the life you want. I want you to be self-sufficient!

It's what my brand Ambitious Mix is all about. My motto is to be self-sufficient and successful in all arenas of your life. It's how I live and it's how I want you to live. Interestingly enough, I've created a business out of this. In today's world, you can create a business out of anything. Whatever you're passionate about, turn it into a business…please.

Since I was a little girl in elementary school, I loved illustrating things, telling stories, and pretending that I had a talk show or was a reporter of some sort. What's stayed consistent throughout all those years? I still love telling stories and giving advice. Once enrolled in college, I decided to major in Journalism. I couldn't think of anything else to major in besides psychology.

In fact, I minored in Psychology initially but later changed that to Communications as I was knee deep in learning all about the various mediums in which we're able to communicate with other human beings. Unfortunately, the naked truth was revealed

to me about mid-way through getting my degree. Having a journalism degree does not guarantee you a job. You'll have to work for pennies and live off of ramen noodles for a while. Hearing that discouraged me a bit, in fact, it stayed in my subconscious for the duration of my college years.

I didn't realize until the end of my college years just how business oriented I was. I often say today, "I should have gotten a degree in business. I would have become a writer regardless because it's my passion but I'm also passionate about being my own boss so I should have played the college thing a bit more strategically." What I mean by that is, with the debt I racked up, there's no way I would have ever been able to afford to pay off my student loans in a timely fashion (as I aspire to) trying to break into the journalism field the

"traditional" way. However, with a business degree, I would have been able to focus on the fundamentals of working in business and building a business.

101

Luckily, I had work experience that I'd gained along the way and anything else that I'd wanted to know, I researched. I worked in leadership positions within school organizations and simply got involved around campus. As a matter of fact, I always found myself in leadership positions whether at work or in school. It was inevitable.

I favored leadership positions simply because I was destined to be a boss and I truly believe it is my purpose to inspire others to do likewise…if that's what they want to do. I'm passionate about both writing and business so I had to find a way to merge the two. At first, I thought, "Of course, I'll be a business writer!"

I figured, I'd write about what I know and share my knowledge as I learned new things. Of course, I couldn't land a job as a business writer because the companies wanted you to have all this experience that's darn near impossible for an entry level grad.

What I did was reformatted my existing blog and decided I would create my own publication.The perks: I'd have creative control over the theme and could dictate the conversation. I'd also gain first hand experience on running a business without waiting to be promoted to such a role. I could work it when I want and as I could. Lastly, I didn't have to answer to anyone but myself.

The whole idea was perfect. I'm telling you all of this because instead of laying down and accepting defeat, I created an opportunity that would give me everything that I desired plus more. I decided that in 2013 and haven't looked back since. It is now 2016 and I'm still looking at ways to make my brand more innovative and engaging. The grind never stops! It can't if you plan to stay out on top. You have to constantly be aware of the trends and changing policies.

Keep the vision in front of you because if you can see it then it can happen. I've made plenty of things happen that were merely just a vision before. Life is very much real and you have more control than you think. When GOD places something on your heart, follow it. He's giving you purpose. You may think, "It'll never happen," but if GOD put it on your heart and you're willing to be patient and work towards it, then it surely will. Trust me.

What I want you to take away from this chapter:

•   Find out what your purpose is and then live in it

•   Anything is possible when you include GOD in your plans. Let him guide you and repeat after me, "The Lord is my Shepard."

•   If you want a certain type of life and it's all you can think of, go after it and work for it until you reach what it is that you seek. You can create the life you want. Stop letting society and circumstances tell you what you're allowed to ha

Chapter 13

May Your Character Preach Louder Than Your Words

What you say versus what you do is most important. Your words have power believe it or not, so use your words wisely. I pay close attention to actions and I deal with people accordingly. If you've ever wondered why your relationships aren't going the way you want them to go then take a look in the mirror and ask yourself, "How do I appear to others?"

What type of vibes do you release when interacting with others? Do your actions directly align with what you tell people? Is your character a direct representation of your words?

Why do people lie?

It seems to me that no one is comfortable with the truth. Insecurity lingers in the air of many while they attempt to maneuver through the many battles of life. The truth will expose how boring they are, or so they think. God forbid, a person attempts to be themselves. "Oh, that's not getting you the attention you desire, eh?" We live during a time where everyone wants the spotlight on themselves.

People literally sell their souls for likes and comments. One can literally become famous by doing absolutely nothing and many have. What mark will you leave on the earth after you're gone? Will you be the person that's known for nothing? Perhaps,

you'll tell an extraordinary tale of following your intuition and God's guidance while living on purpose and impacting others lives while doing so in a positive and productive way. I personally choose to tell an extraordinary tale and so should you.

How would one define **CHARACTER**?

Character is defined according to *dictionary.com* as a:

Noun:

1.   the aggregate of features and traits that form the individual nature of some person or thing

2.   Moral or Ethical Quality

3.   Reputation

an account of the qualities or peculiarities of a person or thing

4. To portray; describe

How are you portraying yourself to others? Does it match what people actually see? Reputation is everything. I remind myself everyday that your reputation is your brand. In prior years, that was not the case.

One was able to keep their personal and business life separate. Now, living in a time where transparency is common and we're so eager to "tell it like it is", we must be careful what we put out into the world whether it's on purpose or unintentionally. Once it's out there, it's out there. The world does not forget because the internet does not allow it to. There's always someone watching and waiting to give their opinion on your life and who they THINK you are.

Building character through Integrity

If you're going to be transparent with hopes that people find you relatable then carry yourself with integrity at all times. You can't be fake transparent, pretend to be someone else, and then be ok with people following a fantasy because you aren't doing society any favors at this point. You aren't helping people when you're encouraging them to following an illusion and you shouldn't be ok with that. With all that's going on in the world, as things happen to you, you are going to change. You'll change without even realizing you've changed because lots of times when people change it's due to a reaction to something that's happened prior.

Practice self-awareness. Learn how to become in tune with yourself so that you don't lose yourself.

"Proactivity is based on the unique human endowment of self awareness." -Stephen R.Covey, The 7 Habits of Highly Effective People

The goal is to be proactive with yourself so that you're constantly addressing and adapting to change. Proactivity is a major part of self-awareness. If we're not constantly working on ourselves, how can we be GREAT. To be great is the ability to realize that we're all human and we make mistakes. No one is perfect and therefore should not be carrying themselves as so. Instead, show some transparency. Show those around you that while you're only human, you're trying your best to be a woman/man of your word and brand.

If you're trying to be effective in your communities, then you should be making sure your actions and words always match, that way people know what they're getting when dealing with you. If you're constantly talking about starting a business, then do your research and start networking.

If you're concerned with settling down and starting a family, then you shouldn't be in the clubs every weekend unless it's with your boyfriend/girlfriend. You can't be in a relationship yet conducting yourself as if you're single. Do you get the point that I'm

trying to make? Your character must preach as loud as your words. It's all apart of you being the best you can be.

To further touch on this topic, I want to expose you all to a website and organization called charactercounts.org. I really love the concepts taught through this program to children in grade school but it's something that we also need to hold on to as adults.

We've already talked about being trustworthy by simply ensuring that your actions match your words but let's talk about the other five ethical values this organization teaches in relations to character. The website also discusses: **Respect, Responsibility, Fairness, Caring,** and **Citizenship**. I agree that these are important values that go into what your brand will define.

We've briefly discussed being human and realizing that's it's ok to make mistakes as long as we address and adapt. What does that really mean though? It means to take responsibility for our actions and by that to correct or find a solution to the consequence. Once again, that goes into being proactive and self-aware. Many aren't self-aware and many times don't know that they're doing the things that they're doing let alone the image that they're actually portraying.

Most importantly, you must have respect and show respect for others. You must also demand respect. Respect scores high in my book. The moment I feel like you've disrespected me, I have to cut it. I do not tolerate disrespect whatsoever and it tells

me a lot about a person's character. For instance, someone that's quick to disrespect another person tends to be immature with a lack of awareness or conscience.

Respect clings on to your reputation so handle your situations accordingly. Nothing annoys me more than an adult who refuses to take responsibility for their actions. I've gotten into several arguments with loved ones over this very thing. Be accountable! I cannot stress the importance of accountability enough. Be accountable and be fair. Treat others fairly.

You cannot walk around thinking your way is the best way. In life, we must learn to compromise and play fair. You're not always going to be right and you cannot make everyone do what YOU want them to do. Believe it or not, you do have to care about other people's point of view as well as their feelings. It goes hand in hand with

respect, accountability , fairness, responsibility and citizenship. Citizenship is most important.

You do not want to be that person that is hard to be around or hard to work with. Do your part as a citizen in society. Be a kind, effective and graceful citizen. You're here

to make a positive difference whether you believe that or not. Your purpose is directly tied to your character. Talk to God and find out what it is.

What I want you to take away from this chapter:

- Make sure that you're presenting the most authentic version of you
- Your verbal and physical should always align
- People can see YOU. Even if you aren't confronted for your behaviors, they see you and are taking note
- Character determines how far you'll get in business

Life After 25: Intuitively Me

Epilogue: *Stay Ambitious, Stay Motivated!*

End of 2016

It took me two years to write this from start to finish and during that time I've learned so much because I've gone through so much. I've grown a lot during this time as well and I must say, I'm proud of the woman I am becoming. In the intro of this book, I complain about graduating from college making under 40k a year and not getting a return on my investment. That was in 2014. It's now 2016 and I've just left a role where I was making over 41k a year but working crazy hours while also trying to manage my own business (that I started in 2015). What I recently learned when I decided to take another position within my company (with more of a regular work schedule) is it's not always about the money. In fact, It's more about your sanity and peace of mind.

I just did something I thought I'd never do to protect my peace of mind and happiness. I gave up the mandatory overtime pay for the work-life balance that we hear about so much but many of us never see. I realized recently, it's not about the money at all. What makes Misha happy? Misha is happiest when she's able to do the things she loves freely without any restrictions. It got to a point where I couldn't even consistently blog because I just didn't have the time.

I'm finishing this book two months late because I just didn't have the time to stay on deadline. Eventually, I began to grow depressed. I was spending time doing something that exposed me to so many things on the daily, both good and bad, for 52 hours a week and it was draining. Especially, when you're not getting what you thought you were going to get out of the situation. Interestingly enough, you get to see how much I've grown with this book.

While writing this recollection, so much has happened and it just adds on to the story. This year alone has brought me so many lessons. Still, unlike many, I did not feel it was a bad year. Despite losing a handful of loved ones to sudden death, my perspective would not allow me to be negative about my personal experiences and circumstances. What it did was brought me closer to God and my remaining loved ones. I'm constantly being reminded that life is short and I understand that more and more every time someone close to me dies.

I traveled a lot within the last year which has a tendency to open your eyes to a lot of things as well. I'm just grateful that I was able to share a lot of experiences with people that I loved and those experiences helped me grow tremendously. Growth never stops. With 2016 coming to an end, I'm sure everyone is on edge. Well, they're sure on edge if they had a similar year as I. I lost many loved ones this year from family members to friends and unfortunately the thing that we must all learn and accept is that it doesn't stop here.

It just keeps on going and we better accept it because at any moment, we can be next. We all have to die one day. This is the one fact that I'm having a hard time accepting since I can remember. I remember thinking about it as a kid and getting sad. I was always a deep thinker. I loathed words like "good bye" and "the end" while always longing for a sequel.

When I think of everything I've encountered this past year, some things many of you know nothing about, it really was a lot but I dealt with it. It was in 2016 that I finally saw the strength that everyone else has seen in me all along. I saw courage come out of me. My moral compass stood tall. My pride was put to the side yet I also saw real anger surface many times. I had break downs like many others do but I dealt with it. I forgave people and I've moved on from it. I definitely feel stronger and nothing can steal my joy. It was a great year of lessons, clarity, and growth.

My advice to you: "Focus on the bigger picture."

Life is so crazy. In almost a year's span, I've had three cousins lose a father amongst other deaths that have happened whether it was a family member or friend, and I've seen others that I know (not related) lose a father or parent. It's like what are the odds of me witnessing so many people (close to me) lose their father? I can't even imagine losing either of my parents. Honestly, I've been praying for all of you and I check on all of my parents as often as I can because that's going to be me one day, (unfortunately).

So, I just wanted to give you all a nudge just to say, even if you don't have the best relationship, check on your parents and work on your relationships with your loved ones because once they're gone, they're gone. I will say that I've gotten so much better at making time for my family and cherishing my loved ones while they're still here. I remember there was a point in my life where I felt a disconnect from my family and both sides at that! I use to reside at a place in my life where I felt alone and skimmed over. I was a lone-star and I had to learn to be ok with that.

I had my group of friends but unlike many, I didn't have many people I considered myself close to. People are fickle and I learned that as I was forced to grow up through situations that have happened between me and other people. The more I went through, the more it changed me. Well, that's my perspective. I'm still pretty much the same girl with the same personality. I just know better now.

I know better of the world. I'm not as naive to things as I once was. I also handle situations differently. It was something about that quarter life crisis that I had. It changed me for the better. I'm simply aging and with age, I've become wiser.

Everyone is not inherently wise. It's something you have to open your mind to. What I've learned over the years and have come to understand is you can literally train your mind to do anything. Your brain is really a muscle.

One can be just as intelligent as the next person, if they apply themselves in the same manner. Back in 2014, I had an epiphany. What's the meaning of life? This very question has been asked or wondered by every single human being that has stepped foot on this planet. I like to think I've figured it out. Everything, this world, the way we see things, our very existences, is all in our mind.

We literally create the experience thus pointing out that we have more control than we think and realize. It was confirmed when I started reading Steve Covey's "7 Habits of Highly Effective People," where he also points out the theory that we create our own worlds when envision things before they happen. We see things play out in our minds before we actually see it happen in real life. Meaning many things that happen to us (good or bad) have already happened once before, when we envisioned it.

Take control of your mind, change your perspective, and find your God-given purpose in life. Guarantee you'll be more happy and will wonder why you didn't take control sooner. Perhaps, it's because you just didn't know. Well, I'm here to tell you that there's so many more opportunities than what you allow yourself. Take control of your mind and stop letting things affect you negatively.

Everything happens for a reason. Trust me. I wouldn't be writing this book in hopes of helping you all if I didn't think sharing my experiences weren't effective in helping you change your perspective. I hope that one day soon you'll reach out to help someone by simply sharing your stories of Triumph over Tragedy. Thank you for listening!

Stay Ambitious, Stay Motivated!

www.ingramcontent.com/pod-product-compliance
Lightning Source LLC
Chambersburg PA
CBHW020916090426
42736CB00008B/654

* 9 7 8 0 6 9 2 8 6 2 9 5 7 *